100 REC...

75% VEGAN

100% VEGETARIAN

4 Ingredients VEGGIE & VEGAN

4 Ingredients
PO Box 400
Caloundra QLD 4551
+61 431 297 923
ABN: 17 435 679 521

🌐   4ingredients.com.au

f   facebook.com/4ingredientspage

▶   4 ingredients Channel

𝕏   @4ingredients

𝓟   @4ingredients

📷   4 Ingredients

✉   info@4ingredients.com.au

Photography: Justin Horsfall www.outpoint.com.au
Design & Formatting: Shem Hunter www.shemhunter.com
Publisher: 4 Ingredients
Distribution: Simon & Schuster, Australia
                       Simon & Schuster, New Zealand
ISBN: 978-0-6484851-5-5

I AM NOT A VEGETARIAN, NOR A VEGAN

But I am asked for this cookbook ALL. THE. TIME.

Seems the world's interest in plant-based eating is on the rise. In fact, it's gone CRAZY! From athletes to celebrities to everyday people, the rise of plant-based diets is here to stay.

Millennials are the central driving force of this worldwide shift away from consuming animal products. But the plant-based movement is bigger than any one generation.

Whether it's animals, the planet or personal health reasons, there is a growing acceptance in our communities for plant-based eating. The change is happening wherever we live, cities, suburbs and country towns. Vegetarian and vegan options grace many menus, far and wide these days.

My goal is to help the growing number of everyday, busy people wanting to increase their plant-based meals. *4 Ingredients Veggie & Vegan* is a selection of simple, delicious and familiar recipes the whole family will enjoy.

Whether you are a vegetarian, vegan or someone (like me) looking to increase the number of plant-based recipes in your weekly diet, then this book is a wonderful place to start.

With Love,

Kim

Guide to Weights & Measures

To help a recipe turn out right, you need to measure right.
I have included this simple conversion table to help, regardless of where you are in the world.

Grams – pounds & ounces

Grams (g)	Ounces (oz.)	Grams (g)	Ounces (oz.)
5 g	¼ oz.	225 g	9 oz.
10 g	½ oz.	250 g	10 oz.
25 g	1 oz.	275 g	11 oz.
50 g	2 oz.	300 g	12 oz.
75 g	3 oz.	325 g	13 oz.
100 g	4 oz.	350 g	14 oz.
125 g	5 oz.	375 g	15 oz.
150 g	6 oz.	400 g	1 pound (lb.)
175 g	7 oz.	700 g	1½ lb.
200 g	8 oz.	900 g	2 lb.

Spoons – millilitres (ml)

1 teaspoon	5 ml
1 dessertspoon	10 ml
1 tablespoon	15 ml

Cups – ml – fluid ounces – tablespoons

Cups	ml	Fluid Ounces	Tbsp.
⅛ cup	30 ml	1 fl oz.	2
¼ cup	60 ml	2 fl oz.	4
⅓ cup	80 ml	2.5 fl oz.	5.5
½ cup	125 ml	4 fl oz.	8
⅔ cup	160 ml	5 fl oz.	10.5
¾ cup	190 ml	6 fl oz.	12
1 cup	250 ml	8 fl oz.	16

Contents

Accidentally Vegan

In researching recipes and ingredients for this book, I stumbled across a FABULOUS blog on www.peta.org.au called "Accidentally Vegan". The name caught my attention immediately, so I began to read.

Now many of you may already know the Vegan range your favourite supermarket stocks. But did you know that there are also a wide variety of crackers, chips, breads, cereals, soups, convenience foods and many other delicious products available that are "accidentally vegan"? In fact, ingredients you may already have in your cupboard.

Here is my "Vegan Cheat Sheet" that I compiled from PETA and also my own research. It is based on the ingredients in the products currently, but products change, manufacturing processes change, so please, for best results always check the packets of the products you are purchasing.

Savoury Snack Items

Ajitas Vege Chips

Arnolds Farm
Full O' Fruit Breakfast Bars

Arnott's Corn Cruskits, Gingernuts, Jatz – Original, Salada Crackers, Sensations Shapes: Lime & Chilli, Vita-Weats: Original*

Artisse Organic Rice Crackers

Burger Rings*

Chic Nuts: Sicilian Herbs & Garlic

Doritos: Original Chips*,

Spicy Sweet Chilli Chips & Doritos Salsa Dips

Eat Rite Wholegrain Brown Rice Tamari Seaweed Crackers

Fantastic Rice Crackers: Original, BBQ, Seaweed

Freedom Foods Chick Pea Chips

French Fries Chips: Original and Salt & Vinegar

Grain Waves Chips: Original, Sweet Chilli, Sweet Chilli Jam Plus Beetroot

Kettle Chips: Sea Salt &

Vinegar, Chilli, Original Plain

Mission Organics Corn Chips: Blue Corn, White Corn

Mission Taco Shells

Mission Tortilla Corn Chips: Yellow Corn, Deli-Style Triangle, Peppery Lime, Smokey Spicy BBQ, Chilli & Lime, White Corn

Pringles: Original

Red Rock Deli Potato Chips: Sea Salt, Sea Salt and Balsamic Vinegar, Thai Chilli and Lime, Sea Salt and Black Truffle

Red Rock Deli Peanuts:
Sweet Chilli and Basil,
Red Pepper and Roast Garlic

Ritz Crackers

Sakata BBQ Delites

Smith's Original Chips,
Smith's Thinly Cut Original

Sunrise Gluten Free
Rice Crackers

Wise Crackers Snacks

Savoury Breads

Abbott's Village Bakery:
Rustic White, Farmhouse
Wholemeal, Country Grains,
Light Rye, Harvest Seeds &
Grains, Grainy Wholemeal

Ancient Grains: Organic Oat
Sourdough Rolls, Apple &
Cinnamon Scrolls, Baked
At Home Wholegrain Spelt
Dinner Rolls, Organic Spelt
Pizza Single Base

Bakers Delight Apple
and Cinnamon Scroll

Bakers Delight
Chia Wholemeal

Bakers Delight Fruit Bun

Bazaar Pita Pockets

Bill's Certified Organic

Sourdough 100% Wholemeal

Byblos White Pita Bread

Golden Hearth Organic Bread

Helga's Bread

Homestyle Bake Herb, Garlic,
Parsley Focaccia

Laucke Wholemeal Bread Mix

Mighty Soft: English Muffins,
Crumpets, Burger Buns

Mission Wraps:
Original* & Wholegrain

Mountain Bread Wraps:
Rice, Rye, Corn

Old El Paso Taco Shells*

Old El Paso Tortillas

Old Time Bakery Certified
Organic Gluten Free Wraps

Orgran Wholemeal Bread Mix

Pane Toscano Pizza Base

Pane Toscano
Pizza Bruschetta

Piero's Italian
Wood Fired Pizza Base

Quattros Pizza Base
Unsauced (12 inch 3-Pack)

Tip Top
Original English Muffins

Pastry & Frozen Savoury Goods

Asian Selection Cocktail
Vegetable Spring Rolls

Birds Eye Corn Fritters

Crazy Dragon Vegetarian
Spring Rolls

Darshan Premium
Vegetable Samosas

Darshan Vegetable
Spring Rolls

Ho Mai Spring Rolls

Ho Mai Yum Cha Cocktail
Vegetable Spring Rolls

McCain Healthy Choice
Straight Cut Frozen Chips

Nevana Fresh Pizza Bases

Orgran Pastry Mix –
Puff, Shortcrust, Shortbread

Pampas Puff Pastry

Pampas Shortcrust Pastry

Trangs Spring Roll Pastry

Rice, Pasta & Noodles

Couscous

Pearl Couscous

Chang's Long Life Noodles

Chang's Super Lo-Cal

Wok-Ready Noodles

Hakubaku Noodles – Udon – Organic, Soba Organic

Health Reflections Gluten Free Black Rice

Lentilicious – 4 Flavours: Lime Time, Turmeric, Red Chilli and Mediterranean

Monika Noodles Chinese

Pasta Riviera Spinach Fettuccine

Polenta

Rice Vermicelli Noodles

Angel Hair Pasta

San Remo – All Pastas except Egg Pastas

Smart Rice Microwaveable Brown

Springlife Organic Instant Noodles – Spinach or Carrot with Organic Noodles, Hot Chilli and Garlic Tomato in Cup

Supreme Wonton Wrapper

Tilda Legendary Rice Steamed Brown Basmati Rice

Well & Good Vegan Cheesy Mac

Miscellaneous Savoury

Ayam's: Red Curry, Massaman & Penang Curry Pastes, Teriyaki

Campbell's Country Ladle Farmhouse Vegetable Canned Soup

Celebrate Health: Lentils Mediterranean, Quinoa Moroccan, Lentils Moroccan, Organic Hart & Soul Coconut Lentil Soup

Heinz: Baked Beans in Rich Tomato

Heinz Canned Soups: Very Special Homestyle Veg and Barley, Spicy Lentil

La Zuppa Soups

Mae Ploy Sweet Chilli Sauce

Maharajah's Choice Dhal Tadka

Maharajah's Choice Dosai Instant Mix (Savoury Lentil Pancake)

Maharajah's Choice Vadai Instant Mix (Savoury Lentil Doughnut)

Melinda's Gluten Free: Sundried Tomato & Spinach Muffin Mix, Tuscan Style Risotto Cake Mix

Raguletto Pasta Sauces: Bolognese, Venetian Onion Herbs and Spices

Roza's Gourmet Foods: Roasted Garlic & Tomato Stir Through Sauce, Sweet Chilli Mayonnaise, Black Garlic Aioli, Dairy-Free Pesto, Thai Pesto, Mango, Chilli, & Coconut Chutney, Tomato Chutney, Tarragon & Mustard Dressing

Slim Pasta: Spaghetti

Spc Baked Beans Rich Tomato

Spc Spaghetti Rich Tomato

Spiral Foods Organic Instant Miso Soup

Tofutti American Flavour Soy Cheese Slices

Dips, Sauces & Spreads

Black Swan: Hommus with Garlic Olive Oil, Sweet Potato with Coriander, Red Lentil, Cashews and Lemon Zest, White Hommus, Hommus with Egyptian Spiced Dukkah Blend

Blue Dragon: Black Bean Stir Fry Sauce, Chow Mein Stir Fry Sauce

Chris' Dips Hommus: Traditional

Cottees Thick & Rich Chocolate Flavoured Topping

Dolmio Sauces: Basil, Classic Tomato, Garlic, Extra Garlic, Italian Herbs, Mushroom, Spicy Peppers, Tomato Onion and Roast Garlic, Farmhouse Vegetables, Extra Garden Vegetables

Fountain: Hoisin Sauce, Plum Sauce, Satay Sauce, Sweet Chilli Sauce, Soy Sauce, Tomato Sauce

Freedom Vege Spread

Heinz Organic Tomato Ketchup

Jensens Organic Pasta Sauce: Basil & Garlic

Kingland Soy Cream Cheese

Kraft Peanut Butter*

Kraft Vegemite

Marmite

Massel Stocks: Vegetable

Massel Gravy Mix Supreme

Masterfoods: BBQ Sauce, Tomato Sauce

Masterfoods: Dijon Mustard

Masterfoods Traditional Tartare Sauce Rich & Creamy

McIlhenny Tabasco Sauce

Nando's Sweet Chilli and Lime Sauce

Nuttelex Margarine*: Kosher, Lite, Original, Olive Lite, Olive Oil, Pulse

Nuttelex Spreads*: Original, Lite, Olive and Olive Lite

Old El Paso Dip: Spicy Salsa Bean Medium

Praise 99% Fat-Free Creamy Mayonnaise

Praise Lite Dijonnaise

Sanitarium: Crunchy Peanut Butter, Smooth Peanut Butter, Crunchy Natural Peanut Butter, Smooth Natural Peanut Butter

Spiral Soy Sauce Tamari Gluten Free

Sweet William Dairy Free Chocolate Spread*

Sweet William 60% Less Sugar Chocolate Spread*

Table Of Plenty: Dukkah, All Varieties

Tofutti Better Than Cream Cheese*

Tofutti Sour Supreme Sour Cream

Vegemite

Wattle Valley Chunky Dips: Exotic Thai with Cashew, Pumpkin & Basil

Yumi's: Basil and Pine Nut, Creamed Beetroot Dip, Harissa, Spicy Pumpkin Dip, Hommus Topped with Charred Red Peppers & Herb, Hommus Topped with Fiery Tunisian Chilli, Beetroot & Hommus

Cereal

Carman's Porridge Natural Fruit & Seed

Cheerios 4 Wholegrains

Coco Pops

Cocoa Puffs

Crunchola Cereals

Dorset Cereals: Berry Granola, Luscious Berries and Cherries Muesli, Simply Nut Granola, Fabulous High Fibre

Freedom Foods: Corn Flakes, Crunch Bars

Kellogg's All Bran: Original, Wheat Flakes, Apple Flavoured Crunch

Kellogg's Cornflakes

Kellogg's Frosties

Kellogg's Coco Pops

Kellogg's Nutri-Grain

Kellogg's Pop-Tarts:
Unfrosted Strawberry,
Unfrosted Blueberry,
Unfrosted Brown
Sugar Cinnamon

Kellogg's Rice Bubbles

Kellogg's Special K
with Protein Plus

Kellogg's Sultana Bran

Muesli, Protein Fruits Nuts
and Seeds Muesli, Toasted
Tumeric and Teff Muesli

Norganic Organic Corn Flakes

Norganic Organic Corn Flakes
with Blueberries

Sanitarium Light N Tasty
Berry with Oat Clusters

Sanitarium Weet-Bix, Lite-Bix
and Organic Wholegrain
Weet-Bix

Table Of Plenty Muesli:
Nicely Nutty, Velvety Vanilla,
Berry Basket, Fig and Plum,
Crunchy Chia, Maple Pecan,
Gingerbread Yumola

Uncle Toby's Plus Fibre
Apples & Sultanas

Cold & Frozen Sweet Things

Borgs Desserts,
Apple & Cinnamon

Calippo Icy Poles

Coyo Yogurt and Ice Creams

Creative Gourmet
Smoothie Cubes

Gelativo Sorbet Fruit
Flavours

Magnum Vegan Classic

Nannas Choc Filled Churros

Nushies Natural Ice Creams

Peters Frosty Fruits Icy Poles:
Tropical Flavour Only

Rio Doro Freeze Pops

Sanitarium So Good:
Chocolate Bliss Ice Cream,
Vanilla Bliss Ice Cream

Smooze Ice Blocks

Tofutti Cuties*

Weis Sorbets

Biscuits & Bars

Anna's Ginger Thins*

Arnott's Choc Ripple Biscuits,
Gingernut Biscuits, Lemon
Crisp Biscuits, Nice Biscuits,
Farmbake Peanut Brownie

Biscuit and Raspberry
Shortcake Biscuits

Eskal Scottish Shortbread

Golden Days Original Sesame
Snaps and Peanut Snaps

Gullon: Sugar Free Choc Chip
Biscuits, Sugar Free Vanilla
Wafer Biscuits

Kez's: Free & Naked Choc
Mud Bars

Kids Outback
Animals Biscuits*

Kong Foo Sing
Fortune Cookies

Leda Choc Chip Cookies,
Chocolate Rum Balls,
Choculence, Dunkies
Biscuits, Gingernut Cookies,
Golden Crunch,
Minton Biscuits

Leda Fruit Filled Bars: Triple
Berry, Apple, Strawberry

Lotus Biscoff

Mcvities: Digestive Biscuits

Munchy Museli Cookies:
Brownie, Spice, Vanilla

Nakd Bars

Oreos: Classic, Chocolate*,
Choc Wafer Fingers – Vanilla
Cream & Strawberry

Orgran Itsy Bitsy Bears Biscuits*, Premium Shortbread Hearts*

Share Pack (Scooby-Doo)

Lollies & Chocolate

101 Rainbow Sherbet Straws

Black & Gold Milk Bottles

Black & Gold Musk Sticks

Choices Dairy Free Confectionery Easter Eggs

Chupa Chups: Cola, orange

Darrell Lea Batch 37 Black & Strawberry

Darrell Lea Twists Black, Raspberry, Grape

Darrell Lea Liquorice Bites Black, Strawberry

Dollar Sweets Decoration Popping Topping

Eskal Noble Choice Dairy Free Dark Mint Chocolate

Fisherman's Friend: Original, Mint, Spearmint

Green & Black's Dark Chocolate

Guylian Solitaire Chocolates

Heidi Grand'or Hazelnuts Dark Chocolate

Hubba Bubba Bubblegum

Jila Sugar Free Mints: Spearmint, Peppermint

Leda Chocolate Rum Balls

Life Savers Pep O Mint Flavour

Lindt: 70% Cocoa Cooking Chocolate, 70% Mild Dark Chocolate, Exellence Dark Noir Chocolate, Swiss Thins

Moo Free: Original Chocolate Bars, Honeycomb Bars

Pez Candies

Select Spooky Skull Lollipops

Sipahh Straws

Sour Patch Kids

Toffee Apples (20g Bars Only)

Ricci Licorice

Skittles

Sweet William: Chocolate: Dairy Free Chocolate Original, Dairy Free White Delight

Sweet William: Rice Crackle Chocolate, Sweet As No Added Sugar Rice Crackle Chocolate

Sweet William: Dairy Free Mini Bar Multi Pack,

Dairy Free Choc Chips*, Rice Crackle Chocolate Easter Bunny, Easter Bunnies Multi Pack, Chocolate Santa's Multi Pack, No Nuts Bar, Sweet As No Added Sugar White Chocolate with Strawberries

Sweet William: I'm Sweet Enough Sugar Free Range: Dark orange, Dark Velvet, Original

Uncle Toby's Fruit Fix: Blackcurrant, Strawberry, Raspberry, Mango, Pineapple

Uncle Toby's Roll Ups: Funprint, Strawberry, Rainbow Berry, Fruit Salad, Variety Fun Pack

Vitality, Well Naturally Sugar Free Dark Chocolate: Rich Dark, Mint Crisp, Valencia Orange, Almond Chip

Whittaker's: 72% Cocoa Dark Ghana Chocolate, Bittersweet Peanut Slab, Peppermint Dark Chocolate, 62% Cocoa Dark Almond Chocolate

Wonka Long-Lasting Gobstoppers

X-Treme Sour Straps

Zappo Sour Straps

Miscellaneous Sweet Goods

Airplane Ready To Eat Jelly Snacks: Orange, Raspberry, Strawberry

Altimate Waffle Cones

Bickford's Chocolate Milk Mix

Bickford's Vanilla Malt Milkshake Mix

Bird's Custard Powder

Cadbury Drinking Chocolate

CSR Sugars: Thankfully the process of refining sugar in Australia no longer uses bone char. In fact, some of the leading sugar suppliers in Australia, such as Sugar Australia, who brand CSR Sugar, openly talk about their process which uses carbon (from coal) rather than bone char to remove any impurities, such as colouring and minerals.

Coca Cola

*May contain palm oil.

Deliciously Free Moist Chocolate Mud Cake Mix

Deliciously Free Savoury Muffin Crepe Mix

Fino Gourmet Fruit Sauce: Passion Fruit, Strawberry, Mango

Foster Clark's Custard Powder

Freedom Foods Pancake Mix

Golden Days Dark Chocolate Sesame Snaps

Greens: Chocolate Brownies Mix, Smooth Lemon Cake Mix, Butterscotch Self-saucing

Liptons: Iced Tea (All Flavours)

Pudding Mix, Sticky Date Sponge Pudding Mix

Hopper 100'S & 1000'S Blue

Melinda's: Passion Fruit Slice Mix, Lemon Delicious Slice Mix, Choc Walnut Slice Mix, Gluten Free Brownie Mix

Movietime: Caramel Popcorn, Multi-Colour Popcorn

Naturally Good Deliciously Free Chocolate Mud Cake Mix

Nesquik: Chocolate

Nestlé Nesquik Syrup: Chocolate, Strawberry and Vanilla

Sanitarium Slice Apricot & Coconut

Sipahh Straws: Chocolate, Strawberry

Soy Life Yoghurt: Vanilla, Apricot & Mango, Boysenberry, Blueberry

Sprite

Table Of Plenty: Dark Chocolate Mini Rice Cakes

Vitarium 100% Naturally Sugar Free Drinking Chocolate

Vitarium Jelly

White Wings Black Label Chocolate Fondant

DISCLAIMER: *Products, ingredients and manufacturing processes may change, please double-check all labels to make ensure what you buy suits your dietary requirements. Also, if you are changing your diet to a vegetarian or vegan for the first time, we strongly recommend consulting a health expert prior to ensure a well-rounded, balanced diet for optimal health.*

Why do you soak nuts, seeds & grains?

A vegan diet tends to consume a lot of nuts, seeds, and grains. These ingredients contain inhibitors (like armour) to protect them and prevent germination until the conditions are perfect. This is a brilliant mechanism while they are growing.

However, when you eat these foods, their protective agents act as enzyme inhibitors in our bodies compromising our digestion and health. Whole grains also contain other anti-nutrients (such as phytates) that can inhibit our absorption of minerals such as iron, calcium, copper, zinc, and magnesium.

Soaking nuts, seeds, and grains (getting them moist) essentially replicates the perfect moist conditions required for germination and neutralizes these anti-nutrients and enzyme inhibitors to make them more digestible.

Foods require different soaking times for full germination. As a general rule with nuts: **the harder the nut, the longer the soak.**

LONG-SOAK NUTS

Almonds, pistachios, and hazelnuts need at least 8 hours.

MEDIUM-SOAK NUTS

Pecans, walnuts, and Brazil nuts are oilier and swell up quickly, so require less soaking time.

SHORT-SOAK NUTS

Cashews, macadamias, and pine nuts have the highest fat content and require only 2 to 4 hours soaking. Do not soak these nuts for longer than 4 hours. Soaking them for extended periods of time breaks down their health-promoting oils.

EAT THE RAINBOW

Eating a variety of fruits and vegetables of different colours ensures the best all-around health benefits. Each different colour contains unique nutrients that are vital for our health.

RED FRUITS & VEGETABLES

Contain nutrients such as lycopene, ellagic acid, Quercetin, and Hesperidin, to name a few. These reduce the risk of prostate cancer, lower blood pressure, reduce tumour growth and LDL cholesterol levels, scavenge harmful free-radicals, and support joint tissue in arthritis cases. Apples, beetroot, capsicums, grapes, pawpaw, raspberries and tomatoes.

ORANGE & YELLOW FRUITS & VEGETABLES

Contain beta-carotene, zeaxanthin, flavonoids, lycopene, potassium, and vitamin C. These reduce age-related muscular degeneration and the risk of prostate cancer, lower LDL cholesterol and blood pressure, promote collagen formation and healthy joints, fight harmful free radicals, encourage alkaline balance, and work with magnesium and calcium to build healthy bones. Apricots, carrots, citrus fruit, corn, pumpkin, sweet potato and pumpkin.

GREEN FRUITS & VEGETABLES

Contain chlorophyll, fibre, lutein, zeaxanthin, calcium, folate, vitamin C, calcium, and Beta-carotene. The nutrients found in these vegetables can help reduce cancer risks, lower blood pressure and LDL cholesterol levels, normalize digestion time, support retinal health and vision, fight harmful free-radicals, and boost immune system activity. Think beans, broccoli, celery, cucumbers, green apples, green pears, lettuce, limes, peas & spinach.

BLUE & PURPLE FRUITS & VEGETABLES

Contain nutrients which include lutein, zeaxanthin, resveratrol, vitamin C, fibre, flavonoids, ellagic acid, and quercetin. Similar to the previous nutrients, these nutrients support retinal health, lower LDL cholesterol, boost immune system activity, support healthy digestion, improve calcium and other mineral absorption, fight inflammation, reduce tumour growth, act as anticarcinogens in the digestive tract, and limit the activity of cancer cells. Acai, blueberries, cherries, eggplant, goji berries, grapes, plums and raisins.

WHITE FRUITS & VEGETABLES

Contain nutrients such as beta-glucans, EGCG, SDG, and lignans that provide powerful immune boosting activity. These nutrients also activate natural killer B and T cells, reduce the risk of colon, breast, and prostate cancers, and balance hormone levels, reducing the risk of hormone-related cancers. Think bananas, cauliflower, garlic, ginger, mushrooms, onions and potatoes.

BREAK FAST

WAKE UP & BLOSSOM.

Nutritional Information

	Per Serve
Calories	136.4
Kilojoules	570.1
Total Fat	1.3g
– Saturated Fat	0.01g
Sodium	19.8mg
Carbohydrates	24.5g
– Sugar	17.6g
Fibre	6g
Protein	2.3g

Acai Bowls
Serves 2

The **Acai berry** is a small, dark purple fruit. It comes from the acai palm tree, which is native to Central and South America. The acai fruit pulp is reportedly richer in antioxidants than all other berries. It's this high level of antioxidants that have made the Acai Bowl a national hero. But be aware, without toppings this bowl contains 17g of sugar / serve. For the average adult on a diet of 8700kJ a day, staying under 10% of total energy means consuming no more than 55g of sugar per day. Everything in moderation!

- **2 bananas frozen (300g)**
- **100g packet Acai Energy (I used Amazonia)**
- **1 cup (120g) frozen raspberries**
- **¼ cup (60ml) almond milk (or milk of choice)**

In a high-powered blender, place all the ingredients.

Blend until nice and smooth (you may need to push the ingredients down onto the blades a couple of times).

Scrape this mixture across 2 pretty bowls and decorate with whatever fresh fruit you have in your fridge.

Enjoy immediately.

OPTIONAL: Sprinkle with our delicious Peanut Butter Granola (p. 34) and a selection of nutritious, protein-packed toppings.

Toppings

Berries, Cacao nibs, Chia seeds, Coconut flakes, Goji berries, COYO, Green powder, Hemp seeds, Nut butters, Orange slices, Protein powders. Sliced banana, Kiwifruit

Nutritional Information

	Per Serve
Calories	323
Kilojoules	1348.9
Total Fat	26g
– Saturated Fat	11.6g
Sodium	192.3mg
Carbohydrates	8.2g
– Sugar	7.5g
Fibre	2.5g
Protein	13.8g

Baked Green Eggs
Serves 2

Jump start your morning with EGGS! Eggs are nutrient rich and are a good source of all-natural, high-quality protein. They can help keep you satisfied longer, making it easier to resist tempting snacks.

- **100g baby spinach**
- **1½ tbsp. (39g) basil pesto**
- **⅓ cup (80ml) thickened cream**
- **4 medium eggs (48g each)**

Preheat oven to 180°C.

Mix together the spinach, pesto and cream, season with sea salt and cracked pepper.

Tip the mixture into a shallow ovenproof dish.

Using a spoon, make 4 little hollows in the mixture, then into each, crack an egg.

Bake for 10-12 minutes or until the yolks are still slightly runny.

MAKE YOUR OWN VEGAN OMELETTE

In a blender, blend 150g silken tofu, 2 tbsp. nutritional yeast, 1 tbsp. cornstarch, 1 tbsp. soy milk. Season with whatever spices and fresh herbs you have. Into a non-stick frying pan over a medium heat, pour the batter, turning the pan in a circular motion to form a nice round omelette. Add whatever fillings you like, spinach, chopped tomatoes, onions, mushrooms etc. and cook for 4-5 minutes or until lightly golden. Using a spatula, flip half the omelette over itself and cook for another 1-2 minutes or until done.

Nutritional Information

	Per Serve
Calories	305.5
Kilojoules	1277.1
Total Fat	17.6g
– Saturated Fat	7.2g
Sodium	36.5mg
Carbohydrates	32.8g
– Sugar	31.9g
Fibre	5.4g
Protein	3g

Breakfast Bars

Makes 8

No time for breakfast? Make these scrummy bars ahead of time and "grab & go" on the days when time just isn't on your side.

- 2 cups (350g) mixed dried fruit
- 1 cup (110g) raw pecans
- 1 cup (90g) shredded coconut
- ¼ cup (65ml) fruit juice

Line a 20cm square cake tin with baking paper.

Pop all the ingredients into a food processor and blend well, scraping down the sides occasionally.

Using a spatula, scrape the mixture into the prepared tin, covering the base evenly.

Refrigerate for at least 1 hour or until firm and then slice to serve.

Store in an airtight container in the fridge.

Nutritional Information

	Per Serve
Calories	321
Kilojoules	1341.7
Total Fat	19.3g
– Saturated Fat	4.8g
Sodium	287.4mg
Carbohydrates	24.7g
– Sugar	2.7g
Fibre	3.4g
Protein	10.3g

Breakfast Burrito
Serves 4

Avocados are a stone fruit with a creamy texture that grow in warm climates.
Whether you are spreading it on sourdough, whipping up a delicious dip for chips,
or a fresh Guacamole, eating an avocado a day is simply good for your health.

- 4 x 16cm tortillas (160g)
- 4 medium eggs (48g each)
- 8 tbsp. (176g) chunky tomato salsa
- 1 large avocado (220g)

Heat a non-stick frying pan and lightly
toast each tortilla until just golden.

Transfer to a plate and cover to keep warm.

Add a little water to the same pan and
crack the eggs into it.

Cook the eggs until the whites are set.

Spread each tortilla evenly with salsa,
top with an egg and slices of creamy avocado.

OPTIONAL: Serve immediately sprinkled
with fresh coriander, basil or parsley.

VEGAN

GRILL TOFU INSTEAD OF EGGS

Drain and pat dry 4 x 1cm thick
pieces of firm tofu. In a non-stick
frying pan, heat a little garlic-
infused olive oil over medium heat.
Add the tofu, cook for
2 minutes, or until golden.
Turn and cook for another
2 minutes. Season with sea salt
and pepper and fresh lime juice.

Nutritional Information

	Per Serve
Calories	204.2
Kilojoules	853.7
Total Fat	7.8g
– Saturated Fat	0.8g
Sodium	115.7mg
Carbohydrates	26.2g
– Sugar	10.4g
Fibre	4.2g
Protein	5g

Cinnamon & Banana Porridge

Serves 2

My beautiful Nana swore it was the warm bowl of porridge she had every morning that helped her live a happy and healthy 101 years.

- 1 small banana (120g)
- 1 tsp. (3g) ground cinnamon
- ½ cup (50g) rolled oats
- 1½ cups (375ml) almond milk

In a small saucepan, mash the banana.

Add cinnamon and stir to combine.

Add the oats and milk and a pinch of sea salt and stirring, bring to a gentle boil.

Reduce the heat, and cook, stirring occasionally for 5 minutes.

Add a little water or extra milk if required to reach desired consistency.

Remove from heat.

Cover and stand for 5 minutes (porridge will cool and thicken slightly).

Transfer to a bowl and top with desired ingredients.

Enjoy immediately.

CHIA SEEDS

CHIA SEEDS *(pron. Chee-a)* are a top source of essential fatty acids (EFAs) which are fatty acids that we (humans) must ingest because our body requires them for good health and cannot synthesize them ourselves. As a general rule, when making a chia pudding, it's 3 tbsp. chia seeds (45g) to 1 cup (250ml) liquid.

Cheery Chia Breakfast
Serves 2

2 tbsp. (30g) chia seeds
⅓ cup (40g) raw cashews
3 Medjool dates (15g), pitted
¼ tsp. (1g) ground cinnamon

Soak chia seeds in ¾ cup (180ml) water for 20 minutes; stirring occasionally.

Pour the mixture into a blender along with the cashews, dates and cinnamon with a pinch of sea salt.

Blend until relatively smooth.

Serve garnished with fresh seasonal fruits, berries, nuts and seeds.

Calories	201.8	Carbohydrates	10.7g
Kilojoules	843.5	– Sugar	6g
Total Fat	14.1g	Fibre	6.7g
– Saturated Fat	2.1g	Protein	5.5g
Sodium	4.7mg	**All Values Per Serve**	

Mango Chia Pudding
Serves 4

2 mangoes (400g), cut into cubes

400g can coconut milk

2 tbsp. (50g) pure maple syrup

½ cup (90g) chia seeds

In a large bowl, whisk the coconut milk and syrup until nicely combined. Add the chia seeds and stir well.

Cover with cling wrap and rest for 20 minutes.

Stir to dissolve any clumps, cover and refrigerate overnight. Stir again before spooning evenly across 4 glass serving cups. Pile high with freshly cut mango.

Garnish with freshly torn mint.

Calories	335.4	Carbohydrates	31.8g
Kilojoules	1402	– Sugar	28.5g
Total Fat	19.6g	Fibre	9.5g
– Saturated Fat	11.3g	Protein	4.8g
Sodium	27.8mg	*All Values Per Serve	

Green Chia Pudding
Serves 2

2 Medjool dates (10g), pits removed

1 cup (250ml) almond & coconut milk

1 handful (30g) baby spinach

3 tbsp. (45g) chia seeds

In a blender, blend the dates, milk, and spinach until very smooth.

Into a bowl, pour the liquid, then add the chia seeds and stir well. Cover with cling wrap and rest for 20 minutes.

Stir to dissolve any clumps, cover and soak overnight in the refrigerator. Just before serving, stir again. Serve with a dollop of COYO and toasted coconut.

Calories	165.7	Carbohydrates	13g
Kilojoules	692.5	– Sugar	9.8g
Total Fat	9.1g	Fibre	8.9g
– Saturated Fat	1.5g	Protein	4.3g
Sodium	77.1mg	*All Values Per Serve	

Nutritional Information

	Per Serve
Calories	303.6
Kilojoules	1266.8
Total Fat	15.3g
– Saturated Fat	1.5g
Sodium	155.6mg
Carbohydrates	31.2g
– Sugar	9g
Fibre	5.6g
Protein	7.9g

Date & Walnut Porridge
Serves 1

OATS 4 HEALTH: Oats are a lightly husked grain, they provide B vitamins along with protein, carbohydrates and fibre. They also have a low GI (glycemic index), meaning they raise your blood sugar levels slowly, instead of quickly like a sugar packed cereal. They are cheap, adaptable and full of health benefits.

- ½ cup (50g) oats
- 1 Medjool date (5g), chopped
- 1 cup (250ml) almond milk
- 3 walnuts (6g), coarsely chopped

Into a saucepan, over a medium low heat, place all the ingredients.

Cook over a low heat, stirring often, until thick and creamy and the oats become very tender, at least 20 minutes.

Add more milk, if necessary, to reach desired consistency.

CARROT CAKE PORRIDGE (SERVES 1)

Into a small saucepan place ⅓ cup oats and ¾ cup water. Bring to a gentle boil and cook for 5 minutes, stirring often. Reduce heat, add 3 tbsp. grated carrot, 1 tbsp. chopped walnuts and 2 tbsp. pure maple syrup and stir. Cook for 4 minutes or until tender and creamy. Serve with additional chopped walnuts and pure maple syrup. Sprinkle with ground cinnamon if you have.

Nutritional Information

	Per Serve
Calories	314.8
Kilojoules	1315.9
Total Fat	4.5g
– Saturated Fat	0.4g
Sodium	631.9mg
Carbohydrates	57.5g
– Sugar	4g
Fibre	2.8g
Protein	8.3g

Vegan Pancakes

Serves 2

This recipe produces really delicious pancakes, fluffy vegan pancakes are possible!

- **1 cup (150g) self-raising flour**
- **2 tbsp. (25g) Natvia**
- **1 cup (250ml) almond milk**
- **1 tbsp. (20ml) apple cider vinegar**

Place the flour and Natvia in a bowl, sprinkle with ½ tsp. sea salt and stir to combine.

In another bowl, whisk together the milk and vinegar; sit for 5 minutes.

Pour the liquid mixture into the flour.

Stir until just combined (don't over-mix).

Let the batter rest for 5 minutes. 'Resting' allows the gluten in the flour to relax and the starch grains to swell, this is essential for light and fluffy pancakes.

Heat a non-stick frying pan over medium-low heat.

Using a ¼ cup measure, pour the batter into the pan.

Cook for 3-4 minutes or until small bubbles form on the surface of the pancakes, then flip.

Cook the opposite sides for 1-2 minutes, or until golden.

Repeat the process.

Serve immediately or keep warm in a low oven.

OPTIONAL: Serve with sliced banana, strawberry, a dollop of COYO and a good glug of pure maple syrup.

Nutritional Information

	Per Serve
Calories	381
Kilojoules	1592.5
Total Fat	20.3g
– Saturated Fat	3.4g
Sodium	21.1mg
Carbohydrates	36.3g
– Sugar	17.7g
Fibre	6.3g
Protein	11.3g

Peanut Butter Granola
Serves 12

This crunchy peanut butter granola makes a simple and delicious breakfast or snack.
It is great with yoghurt, milk, or sprinkled across an **Acai Bowl (p. 18).**

- **5 cups (500g) natural muesli**
- **1 cup (120g) almonds, chopped**
- **½ cup (160g) pure maple syrup**
- **¾ cup (230g) crunchy peanut butter**

Preheat oven to 140°C.

Line a baking tray with baking paper.

Place muesli and almonds in a large bowl.

In a smaller bowl, combine pure maple syrup and peanut butter and heat in a microwave for 45 seconds, or until the peanut butter starts to melt.

Stir to combine.

Pour over the oats and almonds, stirring gently to coat.

Spoon the mixture evenly across the tray.

Bake for 20 minutes.

Remove from the oven and stir, then spread the mixture evenly across the tray again and bake for a further 10 minutes, or until the granola turns a light golden colour.

Leave to cool as the granola will crisp as it does.

Store in an airtight container for up to 2 weeks.

Nutritional Information

	Per Serve
Calories	148.1
Kilojoules	619.2
Total Fat	0.7g
– Saturated Fat	0.2g
Sodium	254.3mg
Carbohydrates	30.3g
– Sugar	7.7g
Fibre	2.1g
Protein	3.6g

Pineapple Damper

Serves 8

- 2 cups (300g) self-raising flour
- ½ cup (75g) Natvia
- 450g can crushed pineapple

Preheat oven to 180ºC.

Line a 20cm cake tin with baking paper.

In a large bowl, place the flour and sugar with a pinch of salt; stir to combine.

Add the pineapple, juice and all and mix just until combined.

Scrape the mixture into the cake tin and bake for 40 minutes or until golden and a skewer removes clean.

SERVING SUGGESTION: Serve with butter (or Nuttelex) and golden syrup.

CHEESE & PINEAPPLE BREAD

Simply add ½ cup grated vegan cheddar cheese to the damper mixture above. This is a recipe straight out of 1965 (except they used cheddar cheese) and is good enough to be served without anything spread on it.

Nutritional Information

	Per Serve
Calories	385
Kilojoules	1609.3
Total Fat	20.9g
– Saturated Fat	16.6g
Sodium	42.4g
Carbohydrates	40.6g
– Sugar	16.5g
Fibre	5.1g
Protein	7.9g

Quinoa Porridge
Serves 4

Quinoa is a complete protein, meaning it contains all nine essential amino acids. It is versatile, carries whatever flavour is added to it and is a great wheat-free alternative to grains. Quinoa is a super grain that's packed with protein and vitamins.

- **1 cup (180g) quinoa**
- **4 cups (1 litre) coconut milk**
- **3 tbsp. (75g) pure maple syrup**
- **1 tsp. (3g) cinnamon**

Place quinoa in a colander, rinse thoroughly with cold water and allow to drain.

In a saucepan over medium heat, combine all ingredients and season with sea salt.

Bring to a gentle boil.

Reduce heat, cover, leaving the lid just ajar so that some steam may escape, and simmer for 25 minutes, stirring every 5 minutes.

Remove the lid and continue simmering for 5 more minutes or until the quinoa has absorbed most (not all) of the milk.

Remove from heat.

Pour into bowls to serve.

SERVING SUGGESTION: Sprinkle with additional cinnamon for flavour, colour and the fact that cinnamon helps your body mop up triglycerides (which increase heart disease risk).

CINNAMON APPLES

Into a small saucepan, place 2 tsp. coconut oil over a medium heat. Add 2 Granny Smith apples, peeled and chopped. Sauté for 2 minutes, stirring often. Add 2 tbsp. pure maple syrup and ½ tsp. ground cinnamon. Reduce heat and simmer for 4 minutes or until tender. Serve over porridge, pancakes or waffles.

Nutritional Information

	Per Serve
Calories	202.6
Kilojoules	847
Total Fat	4.3g
– Saturated Fat	2.1g
Sodium	154.5mg
Carbohydrates	31.3g
– Sugar	25.4g
Fibre	2.5g
Protein	8.2g

Waffles

Serves 2

Don't go out for waffles – make them!

- **2 waffles (34g)**
- **2 tbsp. (80g) cottage cheese**
- **2 tbsp. (50g) pure maple syrup**
- **2 Kiwifruit (156g), peeled and sliced**

Toast the waffles before setting on a plate

Next dollop a spoonful of cottage cheese onto each.

Drizzle with pure maple syrup and kiwi slices.

For a pretty presentation, cut flower-like shapes from the kiwi slices, you can also do this with rockmelon (cantaloupe) or watermelon (so pretty!)

OPTIONAL: Substitute COYO for cottage cheese.

Fat 9.1g

14.5g Carbs

HOMEMADE VEGAN WAFFLES

To make your own waffles, simply pulse 1 cup rolled oats in a food processor or blender until nice and fine; pour into a large bowl. Add 1 cup almond milk, 1 tbsp. coconut oil and 1 tsp. vanilla extract and mix to combine. Set aside whilst heating waffle iron. Cook the waffles according to instructions.

DRINKS

Don't toss fruit out when it starts to go mushy or brown!

MY DAD ALWAYS TOLD US THAT'S WHEN NATURAL SWEETNESS IS AT ITS BEST!

Add them to your smoothies for goodness, fibre and breakfast on the go.

Mint Tea
To increase your daily H_2O intake, simply steep 3 or 4 fresh mint leaves in boiling water for 5 minutes.

H_2H – Healthy & Hydrating!

Watermelon Boost
Serves 2

500g watermelon, deseed+dice
1 Lebanese cucumber (200g), peel+deseed
1 tbsp. (5g) mint leaves
2 tbsp. (40ml) fresh lime juice

Place all ingredients in a blender and blend until nice and smooth. Pour across two glasses with crushed ice to serve.

Calories	97.9	Carbohydrates	30.4g
Kilojoules	409	– Sugar	19.4g
Total Fat	0.6g	Fibre	2.7g
– Saturated Fat	0g	Protein	2.3g
Sodium	19.3mg	*All Values Per Serve	

Green Goddess
Makes 2

1 cup (250ml) coconut water
¾ cup (140g) pineapple chunks with juice
2 cups (90g) baby spinach leaves
1 medium banana (100g), sliced & frozen

Add all ingredients to a blender along with 6 cubes of ice and ½ cup (125ml) water and blend until nice and smooth.

Pour into 2 glasses to serve.

Calories	111	Carbohydrates	21.5g
Kilojoules	465.6	– Sugar	18.2g
Total Fat	0.6g	Fibre	4.3g
– Saturated Fat	0.1g	Protein	2.8g
Sodium	32.1mg	***All Values Per Serve**	

Homemade Iced Tea
Serves 4

3 Earl Grey teabags
2 tbsp. (60g) natural honey (or rice malt syrup)
2 tbsp. (40g) fresh lemon juice

Place tea bags in 1 litre tap water. Refrigerate overnight. Stir in natural honey and lemon to taste. Serve over ice.

Calories	52	Carbohydrates	11.9g
Kilojoules	215.6	– Sugar	11.9g
Total Fat	0.3g	Fibre	0.3g
– Saturated Fat	0g	Protein	0.3g
Sodium	2.2g	***All Values Per Serve**	

SNACKS

LIFE'S TOO SHORT FOR BAD SNACKS.

SNACKS

VEGAN SNACKS ARE PLENTIFUL!

Make our perennially popular **Guacamole** by mixing finely chopped ¼ red onion, 1 small tomato, 1 avocado, diced and 3 tbsp. fresh coriander. Season with lime juice, sea salt and pepper and serve with **corn chips.** Or munch on **Edamame** with sea salt. **Trail Mix. Roasted chickpeas. Rice cakes** with smashed avocado & Herbamare. **Hommus & Veggie sticks.**

Cucumber Boats

Serves 4

Slice 8 Cukes in half. Spread with Hommus or Tzatziki.

TOPPINGS: Seasoned cherry tomatoes, Kalamata olives, capers, fresh herbs, etc.

Calories	70.2	Carbohydrates	4.9g
Kilojoules	293.2	– Sugar	3.3g
Total Fat	4g	Fibre	1.4g
– Saturated Fat	1.3g	Protein	2.7g
Sodium	138.7mg	*All Values Per Serve	

Tamari Almonds
Serves 10

400g almonds
¼ cup (70ml) tamari

Soak the almonds in the tamari, stirring to coat.

Marinate for at least 30 minutes.

Preheat oven 160ºC.

Line a baking tray with baking paper.

Bake for 25 minutes, tossing occasionally, until tamari has evaporated.

Calories	234	Carbohydrates	2.7g
Kilojoules	978.1	– Sugar	2.1g
Total Fat	20.2g	Fibre	4.5g
– Saturated Fat	1.5g	Protein	8.6g
Sodium	337.5mg	***All Values Per Serve**	

Apple Donuts
Makes 12

2 Granny Smith apples (300g)
½ cup (155g) natural peanut butter

Wash, core and slice apples into 1cm thick rings.

Spread with peanut butter.

TOPPINGS: Toasted coconut, Goji berries, dried blueberries, dates, muesli, granola, dried apricots etc. or a combination.

Calories	137.8	Carbohydrates	7.4g
Kilojoules	576.8	– Sugar	6.5g
Total Fat	9.8g	Fibre	2.1g
– Saturated Fat	1.6g	Protein	4.4g
Sodium	3.8mg	***All Values Per Serve**	

Nutritional Information

	Per Serve
Calories	103.4
Kilojoules	432.3
Total Fat	9.8g
– Saturated Fat	1.4g
Sodium	194.3mg
Carbohydrates	0.5g
– Sugar	0.1g
Fibre	4.5g
Protein	1.2g

Avocado & Olive Salsa

Serves 4

- **1 large avocado (220g), diced**
- **½ cup (50g) pitted green olives, coarsely chopped**
- **1 tbsp. (4g) chives, finely chopped**
- **1 tbsp. (20ml) fresh lemon juice**

Place all of the ingredients in a bowl.

Season and stir to combine.

Cover with cling wrap and refrigerate until ready to serve.

SERVING SUGGESTION: Surround the Salsa with rounds of cucumber or crackers to dip.

OPTIONAL: Peel and slice 2 large oranges into rounds. Lay in two over-lapping rows along a rectangular serving plate and spoon the Salsa down the centre.

VEGAN

EASY VEGAN CRACKERS (MAKES 20)

Into a bowl sift ¾ cup plain flour. Add ⅔ cup almond meal, ½ tsp. sea salt and 1 tsp. finely chopped rosemary. Stir. Next, add 3 tbsp. each of rice bran oil (grape seed or avocado) and cold water. Mix to combine. Preheat oven 180ºC. Line a tray with baking paper. Place the dough on the paper and using a rolling pin, roll into a thin sheet. Score into squares and bake 18 minutes.

Nutritional Information

	Per Serve
Calories	174.9
Kilojoules	731.2
Total Fat	4.4g
– Saturated Fat	3.2g
Sodium	287.5mg
Carbohydrates	29.1g
– Sugar	2.4g
Fibre	0.8g
Protein	4g

3-Ingredient Vegan Scones

Makes 16

Hot or cold, lathered with butter, golden syrup, jam or cream – a light lovely scone never ceases to impress. Thanks to a clever lady on our Facebook page who 'veganised' her Lemonade Scones by simply replacing cream with coconut cream ... These are FANTASTIC!

- **4 cups (600g) self-raising flour**
- **1 cup (250ml) lemonade**
- **270g can coconut cream**

Preheat oven to 200ºC.

Line a baking tray with baking paper.

Sift self-raising flour into a bowl, make a well and pour in coconut cream and lemonade.

Using a knife, mix to make a firm dough.

Turn out onto a clean, floured surface.

Knead gently until smooth (don't knead too much or scones will be tough).

Pat dough into a 2cm-thick round.

Using a 5cm (diameter) round cutter, cut out as many rounds as possible.

Knead the dough together again, and cut out more rounds.

Place scones onto prepared tray, nestled up against each other.

Sprinkle tops with a little flour.

Bake for 12-15 minutes or until golden and well risen.

Serve warm with jam and coconut cream.

OPTIONAL: To make your own Jam simply wash and hull 400g strawberries. Chop and place in a large saucepan. Add 250g sugar. Stir well. Simmer over a medium low heat for 25 minutes. Jam will thicken as it cools.

Nutritional Information

	Per Serve
Calories	262
Kilojoules	1092.1
Total Fat	20.4g
– Saturated Fat	10.5g
Sodium	382.7mg
Carbohydrates	5.8g
– Sugar	5.7g
Fibre	0.8g
Protein	12.9g

Baked Camembert

Serves 4

If you want to be the most popular person at any gathering, make this delicious ooey-gooey recipe. It's easy, it's elegant, it's vegetarian and it's beyond good.

- **250g Camembert**
- **60g blueberries**
- **1 tbsp. (25g) pure maple syrup**
- **25g pecans, chopped**

Preheat oven to 150ºC.

Line a small round cake tin, or baking dish with baking paper.

Using a sharp knife, score the lid of the cheese in a diamond pattern.

Combine the blueberries, pure maple syrup and pecans in a bowl and stir to combine.

Spoon the mixture over the cheese.

Bake for 12-15 minutes or until the cheese starts to run and the berries begin to burst.

SERVING SUGGESTION: Serve with your favourite crackers.

OPTIONAL: Combine ½ cup chopped macadamia nuts with ½ tsp. oil and 1 tsp. fresh thyme leaves. Season with sea salt and pepper. Score the cheese, top with nut mix and bake. This is delicious served with warm, crusty baguette.

Instead of Camembert, simply use a block of Vegan cheddar cheese. Top with chopped pecans, fresh blueberries and a generous drizzle of rice malt syrup.

Nutritional Information

	Per Serve
Calories	103.2
Kilojoules	431.4
Total Fat	7.7g
– Saturated Fat	0.5g
Sodium	287.5mg
Carbohydrates	4.4g
– Sugar	2.9g
Fibre	2.1g
Protein	3.2g

Banana Muffins

Makes 12

Muffins are an easy treat for all kinds of occasions. Breakfasts, birthday parties, school lunches, brunch, snacking in between meals or even for a light dinner or dessert. These are dense, but for a quick and easy vegan muffin, they hit the spot perfectly.

- **2 large, ripe bananas (220g)**
- **2 tsp. (8g) Natvia**
- **2 tbsp. (23g) flaxseed meal**
- **1½ cups (150g) almond meal**

Preheat oven to 160°C.

Line 12 mini-muffin cups with papers.

In a medium bowl, stir together the mashed banana and flaxseed meal.

Stand for 5 minutes.

Add the almond meal and Natvia, then season with sea salt.

Stir until completely combined.

Using a tablespoon, divide batter evenly between the prepared muffin cups.

Bake for 20 minutes or until the tops appear dry and muffins are a light golden brown.

Cool for 5 minutes in the muffin tray.

WITH REMAINING FLAXSEED MEAL TRY MAKING THESE DELICIOUSLY EASY FLAX CRACKERS:

Preheat oven to 150°C. Line a baking sheet with baking paper. In a large bowl, combine 2 cups ground flaxmeal, 1 cup water, ½ tsp. salt and 1 tsp. cumin. Spread the mixture evenly over the baking paper about 3-mm thick. Score the dough, forming 16 squares. Bake for 30 minutes, rotate baking tray and bake for another 15 minutes.

NB: Baking time depends on thickness. Crackers are done when crispy. Cool before breaking into squares.

Loaded Bananas

Serves 4

Calories	155.1	Carbohydrates	11.9g
Kilojoules	648.3	– Sugar	7.6g
Total Fat	5.9g	Fibre	2.6g
– Saturated Fat	0.5g	Protein	12.5g
Sodium	18mg	***All Values Per Serve**	

- **2 bananas (220g)**
- **½ cup (50g) vegan chocolate**
- **2 tbsp. (40g) almond butter**

Slice banana into rounds and freeze for about 20 minutes.

Melt chocolate in microwave until nice and smooth.

Dip banana rounds halfway into the chocolate. Top with nut butter of choice.

Refrigerate before serving.

Chocolate Crisps

Serves 10

Calories	151	Carbohydrates	12.4g
Kilojoules	631	– Sugar	3.6g
Total Fat	10.5g	Fibre	0.7g
– Saturated Fat	4.4g	Protein	1.8g
Sodium	98.8mg	***All Values Per Serve**	

- **170g plain, salted crisps**
- **150g vegan chocolate**

Line a tray with baking paper.

Melt chocolate in microwave until nice and runny. Dip each crisp halfway into the chocolate. Place on tray, repeat.

Chill to set for 10 minutes.

Serve immediately.

Nutritional Information

	Per Serve
Calories	316.5
Kilojoules	1323
Total Fat	18.3g
– Saturated Fat	5.6g
Sodium	55.7mg
Carbohydrates	29.3g
– Sugar	27g
Fibre	1.7g
Protein	8.3g

Peanut Butter Cheeseball

Serves 8

What's a party without a Cheeseball? Even better if there are two!

- **150g cream cheese**
- **½ cup (150g) natural crunchy peanut butter**
- **1 cup (200g) icing sugar**
- **½ cup (70g) peanuts, chopped and toasted**

In a bowl, mix cream cheese and peanut butter until well combined.

Add icing sugar and 1 tbsp. chopped, toasted peanuts and mix well.

Refrigerate for at least 1 hour.

Roll into a ball and then into remaining peanuts to completely coat.

OPTIONAL: Divide the mixture into two. Roll into equal size balls. Roll the first in chopped, toasted peanuts and the second in grated vegan chocolate. Chill before serving with plain crackers and fresh berries.

Nutritional Information

	Per Serve
Calories	167.5
Kilojoules	700.3
Total Fat	10.9g
– Saturated Fat	3.3g
Sodium	382.4mg
Carbohydrates	10.1g
– Sugar	1.8g
Fibre	7.3g
Protein	6.4g

Mexican Layer Dip

Serves 8

I love how easy this dip is to make, and how popular it is.
It really is the perfect crowd-pleasing dip when entertaining.

- 2 medium (430g) avocados, de-seeded and skin removed
- 400g can refried beans
- 1 cup (275g) GF salsa
- ¾ cup (75g) freshly grated cheddar cheese

Place the avocados into a mixing bowl,
season with sea salt and cracked pepper
and mash well.

Spread the beans over the base of a clear
serving bowl, followed by the avocado
and then the salsa; creating noticeable
layers as you go.

Sprinkle with grated cheese.

OPTIONAL: If you have these ingredients,
add a little lime juice and zest to the avocado
mash. Serve scattered with fresh coriander
leaves, chopped red capsicum and shallot,
a dollop of sour cream and your favourite
corn chips.

VEGAN

Sprinkle with grated Vegan cheddar
cheese. This is a dairy-free alternative
to cheese and is a delicious blend
of coconut oil and starches.

Nutritional Information	
	Per Serve
Calories	119.2
Kilojoules	498
Total Fat	9.4g
– Saturated Fat	0.9g
Sodium	31.6mg
Carbohydrates	5.2g
– Sugar	4.6g
Fibre	1.7g
Protein	3.1g

Almond & Tahini Cookies

Makes 24

- ¾ cup (187g) **tahini**
- ½ cup (160g) **pure maple syrup**
- 2 tsp. (10g) **vanilla extract**
- 2 cups (200g) **almond meal**

Preheat oven to 160ºC.

Line a baking tray with baking paper.

Place tahini, pure maple syrup, and vanilla in a saucepan over a low to medium heat.

Add a pinch of sea salt and heat for a few minutes, stirring constantly until nice and smooth. Remove from heat and allow to cool for 15 minutes.

Add almond meal and mix until a rough dough forms.

Using a heaped tablespoon, roll the dough in the palm of your hands into a ball.

Place on the prepared tray and flatten slightly with a fork.

Bake for 10 minutes.

Switch off the oven and let the cookies brown slightly in the hot oven for another 5 minutes before removing.

Cool before storing in an air-tight container for up to a week.

Nutritional Information

	Per Serve
Calories	125.4
Kilojoules	524.3
Total Fat	5.5g
– Saturated Fat	1g
Sodium	7.1mg
Carbohydrates	11.5g
– Sugar	3.1g
Fibre	2.4g
Protein	6.3g

Choc Chip Cookies

Makes 12

- **2 very ripe bananas (200g)**
- **1½ cups (150g) quick oats**
- **⅓ cup (100g) raw peanut butter**
- **¼ cup (40g) vegan choc chips**

Preheat oven to 180ºC.

Line a baking tray with baking paper.

Mash the bananas and combine with remaining ingredients.

Roll a tablespoon of mixture into a ball and place on the tray.

Gently press with a fork.

Bake for 12-15 minutes or until golden brown.

OPTIONAL: Substitute the vegan choc chips for alternative mix-ins like dried cranberries, blueberries or chopped almonds for extra crunch.

Nutritional Information

	Per Serve
Calories	173.1
Kilojoules	723.4
Total Fat	1.8g
– Saturated Fat	0.7g
Sodium	234mg
Carbohydrates	34.7g
– Sugar	14.2g
Fibre	1.5g
Protein	3.6g

Raisin Loaf

Serves 10

This recipe is timeless. A stalwart in CWA communities, rural tennis tournaments and countless street stalls. A generational recipe that will continue to stand the test of time.

- 1 tbsp. (20g) butter
- ½ cup (75g) Natvia
- 1 cup (200g) raisins
- 2 cups (300g) self-raising flour

Preheat oven to 180ºC.

Line a 27cm x 11cm loaf tin with baking paper.

In a saucepan over a medium heat place butter, sugar and raisins with 1 cup (250ml) water and bring to a gentle boil.

Reduce heat and simmer for 5 minutes; set aside to cool completely.

Add flour, and mix to combine (careful not to overbeat).

Spoon the mixture into the prepared tin.

Bake for 40 minutes, or until a skewer inserted into the middle removes clean.

OPTIONAL: Slice warm with a little dollop of butter that has been flavoured with orange zest.

VEGAN

Use Nuttelex instead of butter. Original Nuttelex has a margarine like consistency and is made of vegetable oil (primarily sunflower oil 41%), water, salt, emulsifiers (471, sunflower lecithin), natural flavour, Vit. A, D2, E and natural colour (beta carotene).

Nutritional Information

	Per Serve
Calories	203.5
Kilojoules	850.5
Total Fat	18.2g
– Saturated Fat	10.2g
Sodium	3.9mg
Carbohydrates	5.7g
– Sugar	4.6g
Fibre	2.4g
Protein	4.4g

Peanut Butter Fudge

Makes 20

- **2 cups (180g) desiccated coconut**
- **1 cup (312g) natural peanut butter**
- **⅓ cup (75ml) melted coconut oil**
- **4 tbsp. (100g) pure maple syrup (or other sweetener of choice)**

Line a 27cm x 11cm loaf tin with baking paper.

In a food processor, blend desiccated coconut on high until a creamy butter results, 4 minutes; scraping down sides as needed.

Add peanut butter, coconut oil and a generous pinch of sea salt and blend again.

Finally, add pure maple syrup 1 tablespoon at a time, until desired sweetness is reached.

Pour the mixture into the tin and spread evenly.

Refrigerate for at least 1 hour to set.

When ready to serve, slice into sixteen squares and serve immediately.

Left at room temperature, this fudge will melt.

It is best served straight from the fridge, and returned to the fridge if not being eaten.

Nutritional Information

	Per Serve
Calories	153
Kilojoules	640.1
Total Fat	9.9g
– Saturated Fat	6.5g
Sodium	209.5mg
Carbohydrates	8.7g
– Sugar	8.5g
Fibre	0.3g
Protein	7.4g

Sweet Cheese

Serves 8

- **250g block cheddar cheese**

- **80g natural honeycomb**

Onto the centre of a cheese board, place the cheese.

Top with honeycomb allowing a little honey to drip down the sides. Serve with your favourite crackers.

Use a block of vegan cheddar cheese and serve with a generous drizzle of rice malt syrup and a light sprinkling of good quality ground coffee.

Nutritional Information

	Per Serve
Calories	65.1
Kilojoules	272.4
Total Fat	1.8g
— Saturated Fat	0.1g
Sodium	18.5mg
Carbohydrates	10.2g
— Sugar	8.5g
Fibre	1.2g
Protein	1.7g

Watermelon Dukkah

Makes 12

- ½ cup (65g) Dukkah
- 2kg seedless watermelon, chilled and cut into cubes

Spread the Dukkah on a large, flat plate.

Dip the top of each cube of watermelon into the Dukkah.

Serve immediately.

Nutritional Information

	Per Serve
Calories	85.1
Kilojoules	355.5
Total Fat	5g
— Saturated Fat	3.3g
Sodium	4.6mg
Carbohydrates	9.3g
— Sugar	7g
Fibre	0.5g
Protein	1.2g

Watermelon Pops

Makes 12

- **1kg watermelon**
- **1½ cups (300g) COYO**
- **2 tbsp. (20g) pistachios, chopped**
- **1 tbsp. (25ml) rice malt syrup**

Cut the watermelon into 12 equal-sized wedges.

Line a tray with baking paper.

Make a small incision into the base of each wedge, cutting through to the flesh.

Insert a popsicle stick into each.

Freeze for 1 hour.

When ready to serve, remove from freezer.

Dollop each wedge evenly with a generous teaspoon of COYO.

Sprinkle with pistachios and drizzle with syrup.

Serve immediately.

Vegan Grazing Board

Include a variety of dips, crackers, breads, fresh fruits & veggies, nuts, and dried fruits.

LOTS OF COLOUR.

When selecting the options, make sure to select a variety of colour. All BEIGE isn't overly attractive. Include carrot, celery, capsicum and cucumber sticks. Marinated peppers are lovely, as too a selection of olives, cornichons and snow peas. A little hommus and fresh herbs to sprinkle. Remember, the more colour, the more nutrients.

SALTY AND SWEET.

The vegan grazing board has lots of salty and savoury flavours, but adding a few sweet surprises is bound to delight. Try the **Peanut Butter Cheeseball (p. 57), Scones (p. 50), Sweet Cheese (p. 65),** and **Almond Oat Balls (p. 124).** Add a selection of dips and fresh fruits e.g. lychees, berries and cherries and don't forget some colourful crackers.

DRESSINGS

Quick Aioli
Serves 4

Fat
24.7g

1.2g
Carbs

½ cup (125g) whole-egg mayonnaise
1 clove garlic (3g), crushed
½ tsp. (2½ml) lemon juice

In a small bowl, mix the ingredients together. Season to taste. Refrigerate until ready to serve.

VEGANS: Simply substituting whole-egg mayonnaise for soy mayonnaise or Vegenaise.

Balsamic Glaze
Serves 4

Fat
0g

18.9g
Carbs

2 cups (500g) balsamic vinegar
½ cup (75g) brown sugar

Mix balsamic vinegar with brown sugar in a saucepan over medium heat, stirring constantly until sugar has dissolved. Bring to a gentle boil, then reduce heat and simmer for 20-25 minutes, or until the glaze reduces to a syrupy-like liquid (it should coat the back of a spoon).

Cool before pouring into a jar with a lid; store in refrigerator.

Easy Satay Sauce

Makes 1 Cup

Fat 21.3g
11.9g Carbs

½ cup (150g) crunchy peanut butter
2 tbsp. (56g) sweet chilli sauce
¾ cup (187ml) vegetable stock
1 tbsp. (5g) fresh coriander

In a saucepan, combine peanut butter, sweet chilli sauce and stock. Over a medium low heat, cook stirring continuously for 2-3 minutes. Serve sprinkled with fresh coriander.

SERVING SUGGESTION: This is really yummy served with wedges, or a Mezze of fresh vegetable sticks including Cukes, carrot, celery, cherry tomatoes, beans etc.

Green Sauce

Serves 4

Fat 19g
0.4g Carbs

1 cup rocket (60g)
1 spring onion (25g), chopped
2 tsp. (2g) capers
⅓ cup (75ml) olive oil

Place the ingredients in a blender, season with sea salt and cracked pepper and purée to a nice smooth consistency.

LUNCH
TIME

ON THE GO
GOODNESS.

Nutritional Information

	Per Serve
Calories	256.5
Kilojoules	1978.2
Total Fat	22.1g
– Saturated Fat	3.6g
Sodium	26.7mg
Carbohydrates	56.1g
– Sugar	1g
Fibre	7.8g
Protein	10g

Angel Hair Pasta

Serves 4

Most store-bought pasta is vegan, containing no animal-derived ingredients. However, if the pasta has been made fresh, it will likely list 'egg' as an ingredient. To be sure, simply check the ingredients when you next buy pasta.

- 300g angel hair pasta
- 3 tbsp. (60ml) garlic-infused olive oil
- 12 grape (or cherry) tomatoes (96g), cut in half
- 1 large avocado (200g), peeled and cut into small cubes

Cook the angel hair pasta according to package directions.

Drain and rinse under hot water.

In a non-stick frying pan, heat the garlic-infused olive oil (otherwise 3 tbsp. olive oil and 2 garlic cloves, crushed).

Add the tomatoes and toss to coat.

Add the pasta and season generously with sea salt and cracked pepper.

Toss through avocado before serving.

Buon Appetito!

SERVING SUGGESTION: Stir through ¼ cup fresh parsley or basil leaves and serve with a sprinkle of Parmesan cheese.

Most packaged pasta, including spaghetti, fettucini, linguini etc. are vegan. But to know for sure, simply check the ingredients on the packet. Pasta is either made from flour and water or flour and egg. Simply avoid the latter if you are a vegan.

Nutritional Information

	Per Serve
Calories	126
Kilojoules	526.3
Total Fat	6.1g
– Saturated Fat	3.6g
Sodium	151.6mg
Carbohydrates	6.7g
– Sugar	6.4g
Fibre	5.2g
Protein	9.2g

Aubergine Pizza
Serves 4

Eggplants here, Aubergines there. Whatever you call it, eggplants are a low-carb, low-calorie, nutritious vegetable that, in this dish, provides a healthy crust alternative. Bonus, the modern eggplant has been bred to have less bitterness requiring less salting, just slice, season and create.

- **2 eggplants (630g), cut lengthways into 2cm thick steaks**
- **100g grated Mozzarella**
- **4 Roma tomatoes (350g), sliced**
- **½ cup (30g) basil leaves**

Preheat oven to 180ºC.

Line a baking tray with baking paper.

Lay the eggplant steaks onto the tray and season with sea salt.

Bake for 20 minutes, or until softened.

Onto the eggplant sprinkle with cheese, layer with tomatoes and season.

Return to the oven for 5-7 minutes or until cheese has melted and is golden and bubbling.

Serve scattered with fresh basil leaves.

OPTIONAL: If you have Pizza or Tomato paste in your fridge or spread across the eggplant before topping.

WHAT IS VEGAN CHEESE?

The vegan cheese market has exploded in the last few years. These days you can buy literally any kind of vegan cheese; cheddar, mozzarella, Parmesan, even Haloumi.

Depending on the brand, vegan cheeses are made from soy proteins, seeds, such as sesame and sunflower, tree nuts, such as cashew, pine nut, macadamia and almond, peanuts, coconut oil, nutritional yeast, tapioca and rice, among other ingredients.

Nutritional Information

	Per Serve
Calories	234.4
Kilojoules	979.7
Total Fat	11g
– Saturated Fat	6.4g
Sodium	380.3mg
Carbohydrates	18.7g
– Sugar	6.3g
Fibre	3.1g
Protein	14.1g

Cauliflower Nuggets
Serves 4

How good can cauliflower nuggets be? MAKE THEM and you will find out.

- 750g head of cauliflower, cut into florets
- 1 egg (51g)
- ½ cup (75g) Italian seasoned breadcrumbs
- 100g grated 3-cheese mix

Preheat oven to 180ºC.

Line a baking tray with baking paper.

Steam the cauliflower florets until tender, 6 minutes.

Cool before gently squeezing excess liquid from the cauliflower.

Place into a large bowl.

Add remaining ingredients, season with sea salt and cracked pepper and stir well to combine.

Dollop spoonfuls of the mixture onto the tray.

Bake for 20 minutes or until golden brown.

Serve sprinkled with fresh herbs and your favourite sauce to dip.

Good Veggies to Steam

Asparagus
Broccoli
Brussels sprouts
Carrot
Cauliflower
Green beans
Peas
Small potatoes
Spinach
Leafy Greens
Zucchini

Nutritional Information

	Per Serve
Calories	205.2
Kilojoules	857.6
Total Fat	11.4g
– Saturated Fat	3.6g
Sodium	186.7mg
Carbohydrates	15.3g
– Sugar	2.3g
Fibre	2.5g
Protein	8.9g

Mini Stuffed Peppers

Serves 4

These would also be lovely stuffed with **Chow Mein (p. 99)**, **Spiced Beans (p. 85)** and **Vegan Bolognese (p. 103).**

- **8 mini capsicums (180g)**
- **2 cups (275g) cooked wild rice and quinoa**
- **2 tbsp. (56g) basil pesto**
- **½ cup (50g) grated Parmesan Cheese**

Preheat oven to 180°C.

Line a baking tray with baking paper.

Cut each mini capsicum in half and remove seeds and excess membrane.

In a large bowl, mix together remaining ingredients and season.

Stuff the mix into each capsicum half.

Sprinkle with a little Parmesan and bake for 20 minutes or until tender.

Nutritional Information

	Per Serve
Calories	248.9
Kilojoules	1040.6
Total Fat – Saturated Fat	16.4g 3.6g
Sodium	368.3mg
Carbohydrates – Sugar	18g 0.8g
Fibre	4.4g
Protein	4.9g

Nachos

Serves 4

Not your classic Nachos, but inspired by the dish loved all over the world. I have made this 'middle-eastern' version many times, often adding more fresh toppings. Chop up a cucumber or capsicum, add some olives or jalapeños. Sprinkle with coriander or dukkah.

- **8 grape (or cherry) tomatoes (64g)**
- **100g natural corn chips**
- **²⁄₃ cup (187g) Hommus**
- **¼ cup (15g) fresh parsley**

Cut tomatoes in half or quarters.

Arrange corn chips on a platter.

Top with the hommus and decorate with the cherry tomatoes and fresh parsley.

Serve immediately.

Nutritional Information

	Per Serve
Calories	117.8
Kilojoules	492.6
Total Fat	5.7g
— Saturated Fat	0.8g
Sodium	157.6mg
Carbohydrates	8.5g
— Sugar	0.6g
Fibre	6.2g
Protein	4.5g

Smashed Avo & Chickpea Sandwich

Serves 4

- **400g can chickpeas, rinsed and drained (reserve the aquafaba for the Smashed Pavlova see p. 122)**
- **1 large, ripe avocado (216g)**
- **¼ cup (15g) chopped fresh coriander**
- **2 tbsp. (30g) chopped shallots**

In a medium bowl, smash the chickpeas and avocado together using a fork or large spoon.

Add in the coriander and shallots.

Season with sea salt and pepper and stir to combine.

Spread across one slice of bread and top with another.

SERVING SUGGESTION: Serve this between 2 slices fresh bread. As a general rule, one regular slice of fresh white bread has 75 calories, 1g fat and 12g carbs.

OPTIONAL: Add 1 tbsp. fresh lime juice.

Nutritional Information

	Per Serve
Calories	102
Kilojoules	426.3
Total Fat	2.7g
– Saturated Fat	0.4g
Sodium	155.9mg
Carbohydrates	12.7g
– Sugar	3.2g
Fibre	3g
Protein	5.3g

Curried EGGless Sandwich

Serves 4

- **400g can sweetcorn kernels, drained**
- **150g medium firm tofu**
- **1 tbsp. (25g) Vegenaise**
- **1 tsp. (2g) curry powder**

Process the corn until smooth, then add to a bowl along with the tofu, mayonnaise and curry powder.

Combine with a fork so the tofu breaks apart.

Season to taste.

Spread across one slice of bread and top with another.

OPTIONAL: Add a little shredded lettuce for a yummy Eggless & Lettuce alternative.

Nutritional Information

	Per Serve
Calories	232.1
Kilojoules	970.2
Total Fat	3.4g
– Saturated Fat	3.4g
Sodium	906.5mg
Carbohydrates	30.8g
– Sugar	11.5g
Fibre	16.6g
Protein	13.5g

Spiced Beans
Serves 4

This is a really easy meal and has many uses (see below). It can be prepared in advance and lasts well, in fact, some say the flavour gets better with time.

- 1 large red onion (250g), chopped
- 2 x 400g cans 3-bean mix
- 2 x 400g cans diced tomatoes
- 2 tbsp. (30g) Cajun spice

In a large frying pan, sauté the onion until golden and fragrant, 6 minutes.

To them, add remaining ingredients.

Bring the mix to a gentle boil, then reduce heat and simmer on low for 2 hours, stirring occasionally.

The longer this simmers, the more flavourful it becomes.

We love it served over rice, garnished with coriander.

Spiced Bean Uses

Breakfast
Place 3 cups of the bean mix in an oven-proof pan. Create 4 little nests then crack an egg into each. Bake for 20 minutes at 180ºC. Serve with guacamole and coriander.

Lunch
Serve over corn chips topped with coleslaw and a dollop of COYO.

Dinner
Create a yummy Burrito using the bean mix, brown rice and spinach. Wrap and grill or toast to serve.

Nutritional Information

	Per Serve
Calories	219
Kilojoules	915.3
Total Fat	14.6g
– Saturated Fat	8.5g
Sodium	2178.1mg
Carbohydrates	3.7g
– Sugar	3.5g
Fibre	1.2g
Protein	16.8g

Grilled Haloumi with Salsa

Serves 4

Grilled Haloumi - it's easy, it's gourmet and it's quick, but the real reason to try it - it's DELICIOUS **(see also Watermelon & Haloumi Salad p. 119).**

- 120g marinated, roasted red capsicums, chopped (reserve oil)
- 1 vine-ripened tomato (170g), seeded and chopped
- 6 basil leaves (5g), roughly chopped
- 300g Haloumi cheese

Combine capsicums, tomato, basil and a teaspoon of reserved oil in a small bowl and season to taste.

Slice each block of Haloumi into four wedges, then in half creating 8 wedges.

Brush each with the reserved oil and cook in a non-stick frying pan over medium heat for 1 minute on both sides or until golden.

Serve piled high with this yummy heart-healthy salsa.

OPTIONAL: Add some chopped Kalamata olives too; not necessary, but ever so nice.

USE VEGAN HALOUMI

NB: It's not as salty as traditional Haloumi so season generously when grilling. This is a personal preference, but I love Haloumi drizzled with fresh lemon juice when grilling as well.

Nutritional Information

	Per Serve
Calories	66
Kilojoules	276
Total Fat	0.2g
– Saturated Fat	0g
Sodium	302.7mg
Carbohydrates	14.3g
– Sugar	13g
Fibre	1.6g
Protein	1.4g

Taco Fillings
Serves 4

Taco Tuesday doesn't have to be a thing of the past if you want to increase your plant-based diet. Seasoned cauliflower florets, **Spiced Beans (p. 85)**, **Vegan Bolognese (p. 103)** and Jackfruit all make perfect meat alternatives.

- 1 small cauliflower (265g), cut into small florets
- 3 tbsp. (84g) sweet chilli sauce
- 1 tbsp. (20ml) lime juice
- 1 clove garlic (3g), crushed

Preheat oven to 180ºC.

Line a baking tray with baking paper.

In a bowl, mix together sweet chilli sauce, lime juice and garlic, season with sea salt and pepper.

Toss through the cauliflower to coat well.

Bake for 20 minutes or until golden and crispy; careful not to burn.

SERVING SUGGESTION: Serve any of these yummy fillings scooped into a Taco shell or rolled in a burrito with any number of fresh, seasonal salad fillings and a dollop of salsa.

JACKFRUIT TACOS

Jackfruit is a magical ingredient in vegan and vegetarian circles for its ability to be transformed into a tasty meat alternative. Try these yummy Tacos.

Sauté 1 finely chopped onion, add 2 x 400g cans jackfruit, drained, rinsed and shredded. Stir well. Add 1 tbsp. Taco seasoning and 1 tbsp. water and sauté for 1 minute. Stir through ¼ cup (80g) BBQ sauce and cook for 2-3 minutes, stirring often. Season to taste.

Nutritional Information

	Per Serve
Calories	184.3
Kilojoules	770.5
Total Fat	7.8g
– Saturated Fat	2.7g
Sodium	286.2mg
Carbohydrates	17.5g
– Sugar	4.5g
Fibre	2g
Protein	10.5g

Vegan "No-Sausage" Rolls
Makes 12

Ever made puff pastry at home? It's layer upon layer of buttery goodness.
But not in the case of many store-bought options. Many frozen puff pastry sheets ditch
the traditional butter content and replace it with a vegetable oil-based margarine.
Believe it or not many commercially sold pastries are vegan-friendly.

- 2 cups (60g) baby spinach
- 415g can nutmeat, well chopped
- ½ cup (140g) BBQ sauce
- 2 sheets puff pastry (340g)

Preheat oven to 180ºC.

Line a baking tray with baking paper.

Into a large bowl, place spinach, nut meat and BBQ sauce, season and stir to combine.

Roll out both sheets of puff pastry. Cut in half lengthways. Place one-quarter of the mixture down the length of each strip and roll over itself so the filling is encased.

Cut each into thirds and place (seam side down) onto the prepared tray.

Season each with sea salt and cracked pepper.

Bake for 25 minutes or until puffed and golden.

OPTIONAL: Honestly this recipe is a fabulous veggie smuggler. Add chopped onion, shallot or corn, grated carrot or zucchini, raisins and any number of fresh herbs.

WHAT IS NUTMEAT?

Well for starters it is a great source of protein, iron, fibre and B12 making it popular amongst vegetarians and vegans. Largely made from water, peanuts and vegetable protein it is a fantastic meat substitute in recipes like Sausage Rolls, Meatballs and loafs (otherwise known as Nutballs and Nutloafs).

Nutritional Information

	Per Serve
Calories	195.4
Kilojoules	816.7
Total Fat	2.5g
– Saturated Fat	1.4g
Sodium	428mg
Carbohydrates	28.4g
– Sugar	7.3g
Fibre	9.4g
Protein	10.3g

Veggie Burger
Makes 4

There are so many creative and delicious veggie burger recipes, so here's another to add to your repertoire that is meatless, hearty, flavourful and full of veggies.

- **400g can black beans, 95% drained**
- **1 cup (170g) frozen peas, corn and capsicum, thawed**
- **3 tbsp. (67g) pizza paste**
- **½ cup (75g) Italian breadcrumbs**

Pop the black beans (with 1 tbsp. liquid) and mixed veggies in a large bowl.

Using a fork, smash together to combine.

Add paste and breadcrumbs and season well.

Mix all together.

Using your hands, roll into 4 equal patties.

In a non-stick frying pan over a medium heat (may need a little oil), cook the patties for 4 minutes or until golden.

Flip and cook again for 4 minutes or until cooked through.

SERVING SUGGESTION: Serve between a fresh crusty bread roll with your favourite salad and chutney or atop a fresh, crisp lettuce leaf with a round of tomato, thinly sliced onion and beetroot relish.

DINNER

EAT UP. FEEL GOOD.

Nutritional Information

	Per Serve
Calories	294
Kilojoules	1229
Total Fat	12.8g
– Saturated Fat	6.1g
Sodium	899.7mg
Carbohydrates	24.6g
– Sugar	10.4g
Fibre	6.3g
Protein	16.8g

Baked Ravioli

Serves 4

This hearty, soul-warming dish will delight your entire family and is the perfect 'quick' dinner on those super busy week nights.

- **400g Spinach & Ricotta (or Pumpkin) Ravioli**
- **2 x zucchinis (400g), grated**
- **500g pasta sauce**
- **1 cup (100g) grated Parmesan cheese**

Preheat oven to 180°C.

In a pot of salted, boiling water, cook the ravioli until it floats, 4-5 minutes.

Drain well.

Meanwhile, grate zucchini, squeezing to rid of extra liquid.

In a large bowl mix together zucchini, pasta sauce and three-quarters of the cheese.

Into a casserole dish, add a layer of ravioli and cover with a layer of pasta sauce.

Repeat layering process finishing with a layer of Parmesan cheese.

Season with sea salt and cracked pepper.

Bake for 15 minutes or until cheese is melted and golden brown.

Sit for 5 minutes before cutting into squares as you would lasagne.

OPTIONAL: Serve with a fresh garden salad, homemade potato chips or warm, crunchy garlic bread.

Nutritional Information

	Per Serve
Calories	151.3
Kilojoules	632.3
Total Fat	0.8g
– Saturated Fat	0.1g
Sodium	264mg
Carbohydrates	22.3g
– Sugar	5.3g
Fibre	7.4g
Protein	9.6g

Chow Mein

Serves 4

'Chow Mein' are Chinese stir-fried noodles with vegetables and sometimes meat or tofu. My Mum has been making a mince-based Chow Mein for as long as I can remember using the Chow Mein seasoning as a base. In this dish, I simply substitute lentils for mince (because they are cheap and nutritious) and cabbage for noodles because it is a healthful whole-food that reduces down to a soft noodle-like consistency anyway.

- ¾ cup (150g) green lentils
- ½ cabbage (200g), shredded
- 2 carrots (200g), grated
- 40g Chow Mein seasoning

In a large saucepan bring 2½ cups (625ml) water to the boil.

Add the lentils and stir well.

Reduce heat, simmering for 10 minutes.

Drain and add to a large non-stick frying pan.

Pour over 1 cup (250ml) water, then stir through the cabbage and carrot.

Add the seasoning and stir to combine.

Cover and simmer for 15 minutes (adding more water if required), or until the lentils and veggies are nice and tender.

Season to taste.

OPTIONAL: Serve on a slice of toasted sourdough or over corn chips sprinkled with fresh parsley.

Nutritional Information

	Per Serve
Calories	257.6
Kilojoules	1076.7
Total Fat	16.3g
– Saturated Fat	12g
Sodium	282.9mg
Carbohydrates	20.4g
– Sugar	11.1g
Fibre	6.4g
Protein	4.8g

Eggplant & Sweet Potato Curry

Serves 4

Quick. Easy. Delicious.

- **400g sweet potato, peeled and chopped into chunks**
- **1 eggplant (450g), chopped into chunks**
- **2 tbsp. (56g) Korma paste**
- **400ml coconut milk**

Preheat oven to 180ºC.

Line a baking tray with baking paper.

Bake the peeled and chopped sweet potato for 15 minutes.

Meanwhile, in a large non-stick frying pan, sauté eggplant until lightly golden.

Add the sweet potato, season and toss, cooking for 1 minute.

Add the Korma paste and toss to coat ('Korma' is an Indian sauce based on a mixture of spices, including ground coriander and cumin).

Reduce the heat, add the coconut milk, swirl ¼ cup (60ml) water to release remaining sauce and add to the pan.

Simmer for at least 20 minutes, allowing time for the flavours to develop.

SERVING SUGGESTION: Serve this yummy curry over rice, sprinkled with fresh coriander.

OPTIONAL: This is also really nice, using 400g pumpkin and ¾ cup (150g) green lentils replacing sweet potato and eggplant; simply cook the lentils longer than the pumpkin in the yummy sauce, adding more water if required.

Nutritional Information

	Per Serve
Calories	204.3
Kilojoules	853.9
Total Fat	5.8g
– Saturated Fat	0.7g
Sodium	989mg
Carbohydrates	23.7g
– Sugar	5.5g
Fibre	9g
Protein	9.8g

Vegan Bolognese

Serves 4

It is super easy to make this delicious pasta sauce, and best of all, the longer it simmers, the richer in flavour it becomes.

- – **400g can lentils, drained**
- – **500ml garden vegetable pasta sauce**
- – **1 cup (120g) fire-roasted capsicum, sliced**
- – **12 medium basil leaves (10g)**

Rinse the lentils in water and drain.

In a pot, combine lentils, pasta sauce and capsicums.

Heat gently, then simmer for 30 minutes, allowing time for the lentils to absorb the yummy flavours.

When nice and tender, chop the fresh basil and add to the sauce.

SERVING SUGGESTIONS: Serve with your favourite pasta, rice or scooped into a piping hot baked potato or sweet potato, sprinkled with Parmesan cheese (yes you can buy Vegan Parmesan or make your own p. 109).

Nutritional Information

	Per Serve
Calories	348.6
Kilojoules	1457.3
Total Fat	15.4g
— Saturated Fat	11g
Sodium	366.5mg
Carbohydrates	33.5g
— Sugar	9.5g
Fibre	8.5g
Protein	14.5g

Pumpkin & Lentil Curry

Serves 4

- **2 tbsp. (56g) red curry paste**
- **300g pumpkin, peeled and chopped**
- **1 cup (200g) green lentils**
- **400ml can coconut milk**

In a non-stick frying pan, add the red curry paste and fry over a medium heat for 20 seconds.

Add the pumpkin and toss to combine.

Add the coconut milk, swirl ½ cup (125ml) water in the can and add. Stir well.

Bring to a gentle boil, reduce heat, simmering for 10 minutes, then add the lentils.

Simmer for at least 20 minutes or until tender.

OPTIONAL: Serve over rice with Pappadums or Naan bread and fresh coriander.

Nutritional Information

	Per Serve
Calories	344.2
Kilojoules	1438.8
Total Fat	9.9g
– Saturated Fat	0.9g
Sodium	171.8mg
Carbohydrates	44.5g
– Sugar	9.7g
Fibre	7.3g
Protein	15.1g

Lentil Burgers

Makes 6

- **2 x 400g cans lentils, drained**
- **⅓ cup (66g) raisins**
- **½ cup (70g) crushed walnuts**
- **1 cup (150g) bread crumbs**

Rinse lentils in water and drain.

Transfer lentils to a blender, add raisins and walnuts.

Blend until a chunky mixture.

Spoon the mixture into a large mixing bowl. Add bread crumbs and stir to combine.

Rest for 5-10 minutes so that the bread crumbs can absorb any excess moisture.

Form patties and either bake them in a 180°C oven for 30 minutes or fry them in a pan in a little oil (recommended).

*OPTIONAL: Serve these yummy burgers with a **Mustard Syrup** on the side. Simply combine 3 tbsp. yellow mustard with 4 tbsp. pure maple syrup and a pinch of curry powder (Total Fat 0.4g / Carbs 12.6g) or a yummy **Mint Yoghurt**: ¾ cup Greek yoghurt, 2 tbsp. fresh lemon juice, 2 tbsp. finely chopped fresh mint, seasoned to taste (Total Fat 1.7g / Carbs 6.7g).*

Nutritional Information

	Per Serve
Calories	318.5
Kilojoules	1331.5
Total Fat	13.5g
– Saturated Fat	8g
Sodium	1062.4mg
Carbohydrates	36.2g
– Sugar	4.8g
Fibre	5.8g
Protein	13.8g

Mexican Lasagne

Serves 6

This yummy recipe is loaded with Mexican flavours. It's very versatile, you can literally add any number of fresh seasonal veggies to its layers. This dish uses tortillas instead of lasagne sheets for the exact same result once baked.

- 4 x 20cm corn tortillas (284g)
- 400g can Mexe Beans
- 300g jar Salsa
- 1½ cups (150g) grated 3-cheese mix

Preheat oven to 180ºC.

Line a 20cm spring-form cake tin with baking paper, onto which place the first tortilla.

In a separate bowl, mix together Mexe beans and salsa.

Spoon one-quarter of the mixture across the tortilla.

Sprinkle with cheese.

Repeat layering process ending with tortilla, sauce and cheese.

Bake for 20 minutes, or until the cheese is melted and golden brown.

Remove from oven and set aside for 10 minutes. Cut into wedges and serve.

OPTIONAL: Add baby spinach, chopped capsicums and shallots to every layer. As mentioned, this is a terrific veggie smuggler so load it up with whatever fresh veggies you have; corn, carrot, onion, zucchini, leftover roast veggies etc.

Use grated vegan cheddar cheese.

Nutritional Information

	Per Serve
Calories	314
Kilojoules	1311.8
Total Fat	8.1g
– Saturated Fat	4.9g
Sodium	979.5mg
Carbohydrates	44.1g
– Sugar	0.3g
Fibre	1.7g
Protein	13.7g

Mushroom Risotto

Serves 4

It's easy to love risotto; it's creamy, rich, simple and delicious. It also has the potential to take on any ingredient, resulting in a super hearty, family meal.

- **2 cups (170g) mushrooms, sliced**
- **1 cup (170g) Arborio rice**
- **4 cups (1 litre) vegetable stock**
- **1 cup (100g) grated Parmesan cheese**

Lightly sauté the mushrooms in a non-stick frying pan (you may need a little oil to do this).

Add the rice and toss to coat; cook for 1-2 minutes or until lightly toasted.

Pour 1 cup (250ml) stock into the rice. Stir until absorbed.

Gradually add the stock in batches, stirring regularly, cooking for 20 minutes or until rice is al dente.

Remove from heat and stand for 2 minutes.

Add three-quarters of the Parmesan and season to taste.

When ready to serve, spoon across four bowls and sprinkle with remaining Parmesan.

*OPTIONAL: Sauté an onion prior to adding the mushrooms. Serve sprinkled with fresh parsley. If by chance there is any leftover, simply roll into balls, then into egg wash and seasoned breadcrumbs. Lightly fry until golden brown for a yummy **Mushroom Arancini Ball.***

VEGAN

MAKE YOUR OWN VEGAN PARMESAN

Add ¾ cup raw cashews, 3 tbsp. Nutritional yeast, ¾ tsp. sea salt and ½ tsp. garlic powder to a blender and pulse until a fine meal results. Season to taste. Refrigerate to keep fresh.

Nutritional Information

	Per Serve
Calories	76
Kilojoules	314.9
Total Fat	6.5g
– Saturated Fat	1.1g
Sodium	20.4mg
Carbohydrates	1.9g
– Sugar	1.7g
Fibre	1.7g
Protein	1.7g

Pesto Zoodles

Serves 4

In our house, zucchini are a bit like onions and lettuce, they are always in the fridge. I love that they are a good source of fibre, embrace all flavours, and have a high-water content which adds bulk to any dish without the extra calories.

- **1 large zucchini (300g)**
- **2 tbsp. (56g) basil pesto**
- **12 cherry tomatoes (96g), halved**
- **½ cup (50g) grated Parmesan cheese**

Top and tail the ends of the zucchini.

Follow the instructions on your spiralizer, and spiralize the zucchini. *(NB: If you have no spiralizer, simply use a vegetable peeler to create lovely long pasta-like noodles).*

In a lightly oiled frying-pan over a medium heat, sauté the 'zoodles' for 3 minutes, tossing occasionally.

Add tomatoes and season with cracked pepper, continue to cook for 2-3 minutes.

Add the pesto and half the Parmesan and gently toss to combine. Season to taste, serve immediately sprinkled with remaining Parmesan.

Nutritional Information

	Per Serve
Calories	207.3
Kilojoules	866.5
Total Fat	14.5g
– Saturated Fat	10.7g
Sodium	365.6mg
Carbohydrates	13.9g
– Sugar	11.1g
Fibre	3.6g
Protein	4.2g

Thai Pumpkin Soup

Serves 4

Pumpkin soup is one of the most searched soups, and for good reason, it's quick, easy and flavoursome. Here's an interesting twist on the classic pumpkin soup that could possibly become the world's simplest and most delicious Thai Pumpkin Soup.

- **2 tbsp. (56g) red curry paste**
- **500g pumpkin, peeled and chopped**
- **400g can coconut milk**
- **4 tbsp. (20g) coriander**

In a large non-stick frying pan, sauté the red curry paste for 30-seconds over a medium heat.

Add the pumpkin and toss to coat.

Add the coconut milk and ⅓ cup water.

Bring to a gentle boil, then reduce heat and simmer for 30 minutes, or until pumpkin is tender.

Cool for 10 minutes.

Using a stick blender, blend until smooth.

Divide evenly across 4 bowls and serve scattered with fresh coriander.

Nutritional Information

	Per Serve
Calories	352.3
Kilojoules	1475
Total Fat	6.2g
– Saturated Fat	0.7g
Sodium	1398.4mg
Carbohydrates	48.6g
– Sugar	10.4g
Fibre	15.0g
Protein	15.8g

Thai Chickpea Patties

Serves 4

- **500g orange sweet potato, peeled and chopped**
- **2 x 400g cans chickpeas, drained**
- **½ cup (30g) coriander, chopped**
- **3 tbsp. (84g) red curry paste**

Preheat oven to 180ºC. Line a baking tray with baking paper.

Place sweet potato onto a microwave-safe plate in a single layer.

Sprinkle with water, cover and microwave for 4 minutes until just tender.

Transfer to a bowl and add chickpeas. Mash until almost smooth.

Stir through remaining ingredients. Mix until well combined. Using damp hands, form into 8 large patties.

Place on a prepared tray and bake for 15 minutes, turning half-way through.

Alternatively, heat a large non-stick frying pan over a medium heat and cook 3-4 minutes each side or until golden brown.

OPTIONAL: Add ½ cup chopped spring onions to the mix.

Nutritional Information

	Per Serve
Calories	302
Kilojoules	1262.8
Total Fat	14.9g
– Saturated Fat	12g
Sodium	288.6mg
Carbohydrates	33.4g
– Sugar	4.8g
Fibre	4.6g
Protein	6.4g

Vegetable Laksa

Serves 4

- **100g rice noodles (vermicelli)**
- **500g Stir Fry Thai Style frozen vegetables, thawed**
- **2 tbsp. (56g) Laksa paste**
- **400ml coconut milk**

Soak the noodles for 2-3 minutes in boiling water, drain.

Place the laksa paste in a large non-stick pan, cook over medium heat for 1 minute.

Add vegetables and toss to coat in the paste.

Add coconut milk, then reduce heat and simmer for 20 minutes.

Add noodles just before serving.

SERVING SUGGESTION:
Add additional chopped vegetables if you have them, shallots, red capsicum etc. Garnish with fresh coriander.

Nutritional Information

	Per Serve
Calories	173
Kilojoules	723.7
Total Fat	10g
– Saturated Fat	3.8g
Sodium	243.4mg
Carbohydrates	6.3g
– Sugar	2.4g
Fibre	1.6g
Protein	13.5g

Zucchini Frittata

Serves 4

- ½ cup (85g) corn kernels
- 1 large zucchini (300g), grated
- 6 eggs (51g each), lightly beaten
- ⅓ cup (35g) grated cheddar cheese

Preheat oven grill to 180ºC.

Heat a small non-stick frying pan over a medium heat.

Sauté corn for 2 minutes, tossing regularly.

Add the zucchini and season. Stir to combine.

Whisk together the eggs and cheese.

Pour over the vegetables.

Cook over a low heat for 5 minutes taking care not to burn the base.

Remove from stove top and grill until golden, 2-3 minutes.

Cool slightly before slicing to serve.

OPTIONAL: Sauté the vegetables in a little garlic-infused olive oil for added flavour.

MUSHROOM & ZUCCHINI STIR FRY

Technically 5-ingredients but so yummy, I just had to include. Chop 1 onion. Cut 2 zucchini into 2cm rounds and slice 200g mushrooms. Heat 2 tbsp. garlic-infused olive oil in a non-stick frying-pan over a medium heat. Sauté onion. When caramelized, add zucchini and mushrooms, season and stir-fry for 5 minutes. Add 2 tbsp. tamari and toss to coat. Reduce heat and simmer until nice and tender and tasty.

OPTIONAL: Serve sprinkled with toasted sesame seeds and fresh coriander.

Nutritional Information

	Per Serve
Calories	55.5
Kilojoules	231.8
Total Fat	0.1g
– Saturated Fat	0g
Sodium	59.3mg
Carbohydrates	9.1g
– Sugar	8.8g
Fibre	4.6g
Protein	1.7g

Best Beetroot Salad

Serves 4

- **3 beets (246g), peeled & quartered**
- **2 carrots (200g), peeled & cut in half**
- **¼ cup (15g) fresh coriander leaves**
- **1 lemon (100g), juiced**

Into a food processor place the beets and onion and pulse to chop into small pieces.

Remove to a serving bowl.

Add coriander and lemon juice and a little lemon zest.

Season with sea salt and cracked pepper and toss to combine.

Cover and refrigerate until ready to serve.

OPTIONAL: Add some finely sliced spring onions before drizzling with lemon juice.

Simple Slaw

Serves 4

- **250g cabbage, finely shredded**
- **2 carrots (200g), grated**
- **1 tbsp. (18ml) olive oil**
- **1 tbsp. (20ml) lemon juice**

Toss ingredients together.

Season with sea salt and cracked pepper.

Serve.

OPTIONAL: Add some finely sliced spring onions as well.

VEGAN COLESLAW DRESSING

*In a bowl, combine
1 tbsp. pure maple syrup,
2 tbsp. apple cider vinegar
and ¼ cup vegenaise.
Stir and season to taste.*

Nutritional Information

	Per Serve
Calories	39.7
Kilojoules	165.9
Total Fat	2.6g
– Saturated Fat	0.4g
Sodium	275.8mg
Carbohydrates	0.6g
– Sugar	0.02g
Fibre	1.3g
Protein	2.1g

Marinated Mushrooms

Serves 4

- **250g mushrooms, stems removed**
- **2 cloves garlic (6g), minced or finely chopped**
- **½ tbsp. (9ml) sesame oil**
- **1 tbsp. (20ml) tamari**

Slice the mushrooms in half and place in a large bowl with the rest of the ingredients.

Toss to coat.

Marinate for 1 hour, stirring occasionally.

Drain the mushrooms (any remaining liquid can be used over Japanese noodles or vermicelli).

SERVING SUGGESTION: Serve at any BBQ sprinkled with chopped parsley, rosemary and a little lemon zest.

Nutritional Information

	Per Serve
Calories	177.6
Kilojoules	742.4
Total Fat	8.6g
– Saturated Fat	5.5g
Sodium	1456.1mg
Carbohydrates	11.3g
– Sugar	10.9g
Fibre	1.6g
Protein	11.9g

Watermelon & Haloumi Salad

Serves 4

- **200g Haloumi, sliced**
- **1 lemon (100g)**
- **500g seedless watermelon, thinly sliced**
- **½ red onion (70g), thinly sliced**

In a non-stick frying-pan over a medium heat, place the Haloumi slices.

Season and drizzle with lemon juice. Cook for 1-2 minutes until golden. Flip and drizzle with lemon juice; cook for 1 minute.

Remove from heat and cool slightly.

Arrange on a platter with watermelon and onion slices.

Sprinkle with a little lemon juice.

Serve immediately.

OPTIONAL: Sprinkle with fresh mint.

Substitute Haloumi for Vegan Haloumi, though note, it is not as salty so may need more seasoning.

119

DESSERT

Chocolate Nut Clusters

Melt dark chocolate until smooth. Stir through
a mix of roasted nuts and chopped glacé ginger.
Sprinkle with buckwheat and chill before serving.

Nutritional Information

	Per Serve
Calories	256.5
Kilojoules	732.2
Total Fat	0.6g
– Saturated Fat	0.1g
Sodium	72mg
Carbohydrates	40.8g
– Sugar	35.2g
Fibre	1.7g
Protein	1.8g

Aquafaba Pavlova Smash

Serves 6

Aquafaba is the liquid that a tin of beans (I use chickpeas) sits in. It works amazingly in place of egg whites in meringues, mousse, macarons and Pavlova. However, be aware – it does spread!

- 1 cup (200g) caster sugar
- 1½ tbsp. (15g) arrowroot
- 400g can chickpeas, chilled
- 1 tsp. (5ml) apple cider vinegar

Preheat the oven to 135ºC.

Line a baking tray with baking paper and onto it, draw a 15cm circle. In a small bowl, mix together the sugar, arrowroot and a good pinch of sea salt. Set aside.

Pour the chilled chickpea liquid (aquafaba) into the bowl of a stand mixer. Add the apple cider vinegar and beat on low, gradually increasing the speed to high for 4-5 minutes or until the liquid is fluffy, tripled in size, and soft peaks have formed.

Reduce the speed and start adding the sugar gradually, 1 tablespoon at a time.

Once all of the sugar has been added, increase the speed to high and beat until stiff, glossy peaks form and hold their shape, 10-12 minutes.

Using a spatula, pile the mixture into the drawn circle, knowing it will fall and spread.

Place in the lower third of the oven and reduce the temperature to 120ºC.

Bake for 2½ hours, or until the outside is dry to the touch. Turn the oven off and leave the pavlova inside to cool completely.

OPTIONAL: Serve with whipped coconut cream or COYO and a smattering of fresh berries, passion fruit and pistachios.
To create our Pavlova Smash, break up and scatter across a platter before decorating with various toppings.

Nutritional Information

	Per Serve
Calories	68.8
Kilojoules	287.8
Total Fat	4.4g
– Saturated Fat	0.3g
Sodium	0.5mg
Carbohydrates	4.9g
– Sugar	2.6g
Fibre	1.4g
Protein	2g

Almond Oat Balls

Makes 12

- **8 Medjool dates (40g), pitted**
- **4 tbsp. (64g) almond butter**
- **½ cup (50g) oats**
- **2 tbsp. (22g) slivered almonds, crushed**

Into a food processor place the dates and pulse to break up.

Add remaining ingredients.

Blend to combine.

Using a tablespoon of mixture, roll into balls.

Place in freezer to set for about 10 minutes then store in an airtight container in the fridge for up to 7 days.

OPTIONAL: Add a mixture of dried dates and dried figs.

Nutritional Information

	Per Serve
Calories	82.6
Kilojoules	345.1
Total Fat	5.9g
– Saturated Fat	2.8g
Sodium	7.5mg
Carbohydrates	5.8g
– Sugar	4.2g
Fibre	1.4g
Protein	1.2g

Avocado Choc Truffles

Makes 16

- **1 ripe avocado (200g)**
- **2 tbsp. (25g) brown sugar**
- **2 tbsp. (15g) raw cocoa powder (extra for rolling)**
- **140g vegan chocolate, chopped**

Pit the avocado and mash the flesh with a fork until completely smooth and lump free.

Add the brown sugar, cocoa powder and season with sea salt; stir to combine.

In a microwave-safe bowl, melt the chocolate in 30-second increments, stirring after each until nice and runny.

Once melted, pour into avocado mixture and stir until thoroughly combined.

Refrigerate for at least 1 hour to set.

Using a teaspoon, form the mixture into balls with your hands and place on a plate.

Repeat with remaining mixture.

Sift extra cocoa powder over the top, rolling to completely cover.

Refrigerate until ready to serve (you may need to roll again on the plate to recover with cacao powder).

Nutritional Information

	Per Serve
Calories	269.6
Kilojoules	1126.8
Total Fat	10.3g
– Saturated Fat	1.2g
Sodium	586.3mg
Carbohydrates	38.1g
– Sugar	8.7g
Fibre	1.4g
Protein	4.5g

Banana Bread

Serves 8

- **2 large, really ripe bananas (300g)**
- **½ cup (75g) Natvia**
- **1 cup (260g) whole-egg mayonnaise**
- **2 cups (300g) self-raising flour**

Preheat oven to 180°C.

Line a 27cm x 11cm loaf tin with baking paper.

In a medium bowl, mash the bananas. Stir in the Natvia, add the mayonnaise, pinch of sea salt and flour, and lightly mix, just to combine.

Using a spatula, scrape the mixture into the tin and bake until a skewer inserted into the centre comes out clean, 45 minutes.

Let cool in the tin for 15 minutes.

Enjoy warm immediately or lightly grilled the next day with jam for breakfast.

OPTIONAL: Before baking, sprinkle generously with ground spices e.g. cinnamon and nutmeg. In addition to adding flavour, spices also add health benefits too.

Use Vegenaise or PRAISE 99% Fat-Free Creamy Mayonnaise instead of whole-egg mayonnaise. The big difference between both are eggs. Obviously whole-egg uses eggs, where many Vegan mayos use vegetable proteins (e.g. soy) instead of eggs. The main ingredients found in Vegenaise are mustard, oil, apple cider vinegar, soy protein, brown rice syrup, salt, and lemon juice.

Nutritional Information

	Per Serve
Calories	364.8
Kilojoules	1524.9
Total Fat	28g
– Saturated Fat	1.7g
Sodium	18.5mg
Carbohydrates	15.1g
– Sugar	12.4g
Fibre	6.6g
Protein	11g

Carrot Cake
Serves 8

- **2 carrots (170g), ends trimmed, grated**
- **12 Medjool dates (60g), halved, deseeded**
- **2 ripe bananas (220g)**
- **4 cups (400g) almond meal**

Preheat oven to 180ºC.

Line a 20cm cake tin with baking paper (or a 27cm x 11cm loaf tin).

Place the carrots and dates into a food processor and blend until sticky and well combined. You will need to stop, scrape down the sides and pulse several times.

Meanwhile, in a large bowl mash the banana to a smooth paste.

Add almond meal and carrot mixture; stir until just combined.

Spoon the mixture into the cake tin, level the lid lightly with the back of a spoon.

Bake for 45 minutes.

Remove from the oven and cool for 10 minutes.

OPTIONAL: Use only 2 cups of almond meal + 2 cups desiccated coconut. This not only reduces the cost of the cake, but adds a really lovely flavour to it. NB: This cake does not rise but results in a lovely moist cake.

VEGAN CREAM CHEESE FROSTING

In a bowl, combine 2 tbsp. room temperature Nuttelex (or vegan butter) + 125g vegan cream cheese and 2 cups sifted icing sugar. Beat to combine. You may need to add more icing sugar to reach the right consistency. A little splash of lemon juice would be lovely too.

Nutritional Information

	Per Serve
Calories	380.3
Kilojoules	1589.8
Total Fat	25.9g
– Saturated Fat	15.9g
Sodium	49.9mg
Carbohydrates	26g
– Sugar	22.6g
Fibre	0.6g
Protein	8.9g

Chocolate Fudge Torte
Serves 8

This simple chocolate torte is foolproof, impressive, and incredibly decadent.

- 400g 70% dark chocolate, broken
- 1 cup (250ml) coconut milk
- ⅓ cup (106g) pure maple syrup
- 4 eggs (51g each)

Preheat oven to 150ºC.

Lightly spray a 20cm flan tin with coconut oil spray.

In a microwaveable bowl, place chocolate, coconut milk and pure maple syrup.

Heat in 30-second increments, stirring after each until nice and smooth.

Set aside to cool.

Whisk the eggs well.

Add to the chocolate mixture and fold to combine.

Pour into flan tin and bake for 50 minutes or until a skewer inserted into the centre removes clean.

SERVING SUGGESTION: This is a deliciously rich torte, so to compliment, serve dusted with pure icing sugar, berries and a dollop of cream or a scoop of creamy, vanilla ice-cream.

OPTIONAL: I added a ½ tsp. of pure almond extract for a lovely twist.

Nutritional Information

	Per Serve
Calories	145.1
Kilojoules	606.5
Total Fat	4.9g
– Saturated Fat	2.6g
Sodium	81.3mg
Carbohydrates	14.2g
– Sugar	6g
Fibre	0.8g
Protein	11g

Cookies & Cream Truffles
Makes 16

The ingredients on the packet of Oreos I'm looking at are as follows: *sugar, unbleached enriched flour, high oleic canola and/or palm and/or canola oil, cocoa, high fructose corn syrup, leavening, cornflour, salt, soy lecithin and vanillin.* Nothing glaringly offensive to vegans there. However, as with many manufacturers that produce other products 'cross-contamination' may mean that two different products may be made on the same machine. So in this case, Oreos can't be quality-controlled for traces of milk. If you don't want to take the chance, don't make this recipe. If, however, you are like me and aren't that strict – **THEN, YOU ARE WELCOME** – these will change your life!

- 2 x 150g packets Oreos cookies
- 75g vegan cream cheese
- 200g vegan chocolate (or chocolate of choice)

Line a tray with baking paper.

In a food processor blend all but 2 of the cookies into a fine meal (this may need to be done in batches depending on the strength of your blender).

Add the cream cheese and beat together until no traces of white remain.

The dough should be thick enough to roll together easily. Roll a tablespoon of mixture into a ball and place on the tray. Chill when all are done.

Meanwhile, break the vegan chocolate into a ceramic bowl and microwave on high in 30-second increments until nice and smooth.

Crumble the remaining 2 Oreo biscuits.

Using forks, dip each of the Oreo balls into the chocolate, allowing excess chocolate to drip back into the bowl.

Place back on the tray, sprinkle lightly with Oreo crumble and refrigerate when all are done.

Melt a little white chocolate and use it to drizzle across every second ball for a nice contrast.

Nutritional Information

	Per Serve
Calories	301.5
Kilojoules	1260.1
Total Fat	0.8g
– Saturated Fat	0.1g
Sodium	219.7mg
Carbohydrates	68.7g
– Sugar	46.7g
Fibre	3.5g
Protein	4.6g

Mango Fruit Cake
Serves 16

This fruit cake will be the star attraction at any gathering. It's that unexpected burst of deliciously, slowly baked mango that is the real surprise here.

- **1kg mixed dried fruit**
- **800g can mangoes**
- **3 cups (450g) self-raising flour**

Into a large bowl place the mixed dried fruit.

Pour over the can of mangoes, fruit and all the juice. Stir well and leave for at least 2 hours, I often leave covered overnight.

Preheat oven to 125ºC.

Line a 22cm cake tin with baking paper.

Add the self-raising flour and stir to combine.

Spoon the mixture into the tin.

In the lower half of the oven, bake for 2 ½ - 3 hours or until a skewer inserted into the centre of the cake removes clean.

Set aside to cool before turning out.

SILKY SMOOTH
BUTTERCREAM FROSTING

*Into a large bowl place
3½ cups pure icing sugar.
Add 1 cup Nuttelex, a pinch of
sea salt and 1 tsp. vanilla extract.
Using electric beaters, beat until
thick and smooth. If consistency is
too thick, add 1 tbsp. coconut milk.
If consistency too thin, add more
icing sugar.*

Nutritional Information

	Per Serve
Calories	418.5
Kilojoules	1749.3
Total Fat	13.2g
– Saturated Fat	10.7g
Sodium	25.8mg
Carbohydrates	68.8g
– Sugar	28g
Fibre	1.9g
Protein	5.6g

Thai Mango Sticky Rice Pudding
Serves 4

A vegan sticky rice pudding, the perfect creamy, comfort dessert.

- **1 cup (200g) long grain rice**
- **4 tbsp. (50g) brown sugar**
- **400ml can coconut milk (not lite)**
- **2 ripe mangoes (450g)**

In a saucepan, soak the rice in 1 cup (250ml) water for 20-30 minutes; do not drain.

Add ½ cup (125ml) more water, plus ½ can coconut milk, ¼ tsp. sea salt and 1 tbsp. brown sugar. Stir well.

Bring to a gentle boil, then partially cover with a lid (leaving room for steam to escape).

Reduce heat and simmer for 20 minutes, or until most of the liquid has been absorbed by the rice and rice is tender.

Turn off the heat, but leave the pan on the stove top with the lid on tight.

Sit for 10 minutes.

To make the sauce, warm (do not boil) the rest of the coconut milk over medium-low heat, 5 minutes.

Add 3 tablespoons brown sugar, stirring to dissolve *(NB: It will taste less sweet when added to the rice.)*

Prepare the mangoes by cutting it open and slicing into bite-size pieces.

Scoop some warm rice into each serving bowl or glass, then pour the sweet coconut sauce over each.

Arrange mango cubes on the rice and drizzle with more sauce.

Serve immediately.

IT'S A DATE!

We LOVE stuffed dates. They are easy to make (no oven required), deliciously decadent to eat, there are numerous ways to make them, and you can prepare as many or as few as you like. **Dates are easy entertaining at its best!**

Surprise Date
Makes 10

10 Medjool dates (50g)
4 tbsp. (80g) cream cheese
2 tbsp. (32g) pure icing sugar
1 tbsp. (22g) caramelised balsamic glaze

Slice each date lengthwise and remove the pit.

Mix cream cheese and icing sugar together.

Spoon into the dates.

Place on a serving plate and drizzle with caramelized balsamic glaze to serve immediately.

Fat
2.3g

7.9g
Carbs

Chocolate Pretzel Date

Stuff each date with a pretzel stick (or any number of broken pretzels) and drizzle with dark chocolate.
That's it!

Fat
2.1g

10g
Carbs

Dinner Date

Stuff the date with a slice of brie and a pecan.

Fat
2.1g

3.6g
Carbs

Romantic Date
Makes 10

10 Medjool dates
4 tbsp. cream cheese
1 tbsp. natural honey
¼ cup (35g) salted, roasted almonds, chopped

Slice each date lengthwise and remove the pit.

Mix cream cheese and natural honey together.

Spoon into the dates.

Place on a serving plate and sprinkle generously with the chopped almonds.

Fat
3.9g

6g
Carbs

Tiramisu Date
Makes 10

10 Medjool dates (50g)
4 tbsp. (80g) mascarpone (or cream cheese)
1 tbsp. (28g) natural honey
2 tbsp. (42g) finely ground coffee

Slice each date lengthwise and remove the pit.

Mix together mascarpone and natural honey.

Spoon into the dates. Spread the coffee over a plate.

Roll each date in the coffee.

Fat
2.3g

6.3g
Carbs

Retro Date
Makes 1

10 Medjool dates
3 tbsp. (50g) goats cheese
5 semi-dried tomatoes (25g), chopped
6 fresh basil leaves (5g)

Slice each date lengthwise and remove the pit.

Fill each date with equal parts goat cheese and semi-dried tomato. To chiffonade basil, stack the fresh leaves on top of each other and gently roll into a cigar. Use a sharp knife to slice into thin ribbons.

Serve these dates sprinkled with the basil.

Fat
2g

3.5g
Carbs

Please Join Us

4 Ingredients is a family of busy people bound together by the desire to create good, healthy, homemade meals quickly, easily and economically.

Our aim is to save us all precious time and money in the kitchen. If this is you too, then we invite you to join our growing family where we share kitchen wisdom daily.

Similarly, if you have a favourite recipe or a tip that has worked for you in the kitchen and think others would enjoy it too, we'd love to hear from you:

 facebook.com/4ingredientspage

4 Ingredients Channel

@4ingredients

@4ingredients

@4ingredients

4ingredients.com.au

Bibliography

Websites

ACCIDENTALLY VEGAN
https://www.peta.org.au/living/
accidentally-vegan/

VEGAN TRENDS
https://www.vegansociety.com/
news/media/statistics

MOST GOOGLED 2019
https://www.goodfood.com.au/recipes/
news/australias-10-most-googled-recipes-
of-2019-20191211-h1kbgw

Why do you soak nuts, seeds, and grains
https://www.theblendergirl.com/hint-tip/
soaking-nuts-seeds-grains/

EAT THE RAINBOW
https://www.lifeeducation.org.au/parents/
eating-the-rainbow?

Books & Magazines

McCosker, Kim. **4 Ingredients KETO.**
4 Ingredients. PO BOX 400. Caloundra
Queensland 4551. Australia.

McCosker, Kim. **4 Ingredients Healthy Diet.**
4 Ingredients. PO BOX 400. Caloundra
Queensland 4551. Australia.

McCosker, Kim. **4 Ingredients MORE Gluten
Free Lactose Free.** 4 Ingredients. PO BOX 400.
Caloundra Queensland 4551. Australia.

Von Euw, Emily. **RAWSOME VEGAN BAKING.**
Page Street Publishing. 27 Congress Street,
Suite 103. Salem, MA 01970.

**LOVE FOOD. VEGETARIAN - 150 Inspired ideas
for everyday cooking.** Parragon Books Ltd.
Chartist House. 15-17 Trim Street. Bath BA1
1HA, UK.

Index

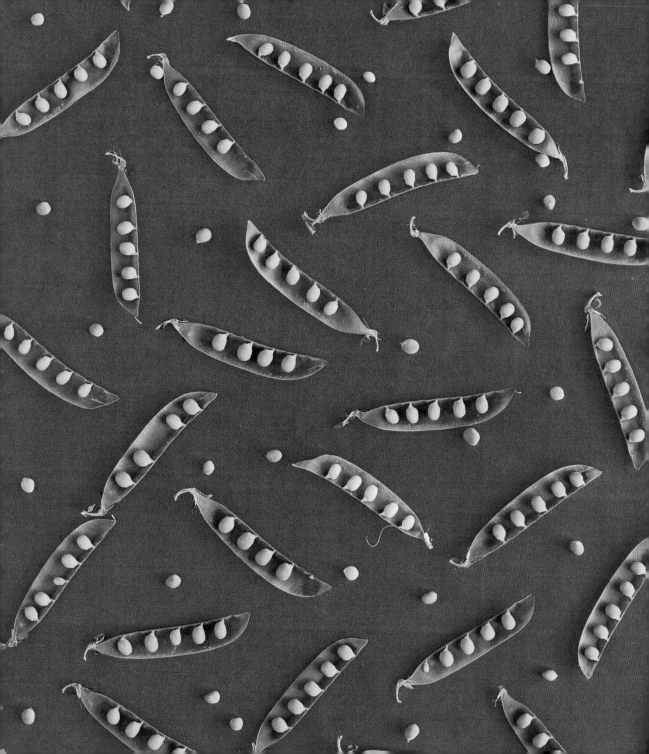